MY WELSH MASTERS

Map of Wales with the 13 old counties

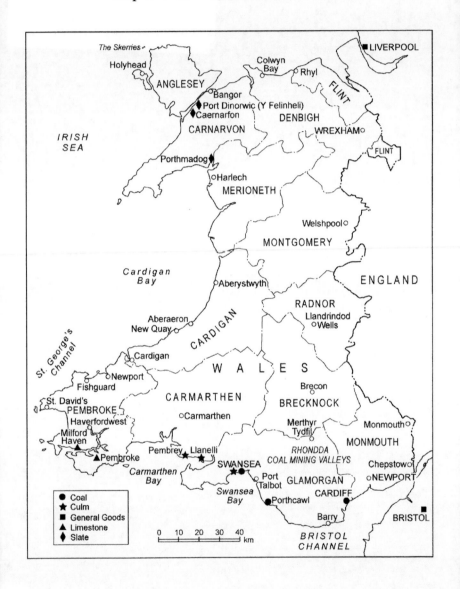

MY WELSH MASTERS

LEN DAVIES

For permission to reprint or broadcast
please contact the author by email:

l.davies417@btinternet.com

ISBN-13 978-1511956215

Typeset & Design by GWCS

Cover Illustration by Geoff Scott

INTRODUCTION

Cardigan began to grow in importance as a port in the early sixteenth century, becoming second only in importance to Milford by the eighteenth and nineteenth centuries. It had its Customs House with responsibility to collect taxes from any maritime trade occurring not only in its port but also at any other small port, beach or landing place on this coastline, stretching from Aberaeron to Fishguard.

There was both foreign and coastal trade, with the latter the most prevalent. Most beaches saw some maritime trade during this time, mainly the landing of coal, culm, and limestone. A few, such as Aberporth, had a thriving fishing industry that included the salting and smoking of herring. Many others saw some shipbuilding activity, with New Quay and Cardigan the most predominant.

Indeed, the maritime trade at the port of Cardigan was vital to the development and economy, not only of Cardigan itself but also its hinterland. Understandably, there developed the tradition of a large proportion of the male population earning a living for themselves and their families from this maritime trade, be it as ship owners, merchants, sailors, shipbuilders, sail makers, rope makers or one of the many other allied trades that existed.

This book is the story of one such family (who happen to be my ancestors), who from humble beginnings went on to become sailors, master mariners, ship owners, and investors.

A Seafaring Family

John Davies was born in 1803 just to the north of Cardigan; his father was a farm labourer. He went to sea as an apprentice at the age of sixteen and became a master mariner, ship owner, and investor in ships, retaining an association with the sea until his death in 1886. He married a sailor's daughter and settled in the village of St Dogmaels where they had eight children.

Of these children one daughter died in infancy, while three sons went to sea and became master mariners. Two of their daughters married master mariners, one married a ship's carpenter, and one married a building contractor and farmer. Many of their children's children became sailors and master mariners themselves. As Cardigan saw the decline of its port through the second half of the nineteenth century, the tradition of men from this stretch of coastline going to sea continued into the twentieth, only now they were sailing from ports such as Cardiff and Liverpool, as did the sailors of this family.

This book highlights some of their successes and disappointments: a birth at sea, deaths at sea from accidents, disease and war, courage, duty to family and employer, burning ambition, desperate bad luck and sometimes well-earned good fortune. In short, it is a brief look back through time into their daily lives, whether on the ever-developing land or the turbulent sea.

A Word of Thanks

I am indebted to staff at the County Record Offices at Haverfordwest, Aberystwyth; The National Library of Wales Aberystwyth; Cardigan Library; West Glamorgan Archives Service Swansea, and the Glamorgan Archives Cardiff for their help and advice, enabling me to consult a variety of documents and records over a period of many years of research. My grateful thanks are also extended to the staff at the Public Record Office Kew, the National Maritime Museum Greenwich, the London Metropolitan Archives, and Cambridge Central Library for their informed help and advice also over many years.

I would also like to sincerely thank the many individuals who have talked to me enthusiastically in person, by telephone and by e-mail, a process that has given me an enormous amount of information regarding this family, without which I could not have completed this book.

My grateful thanks are therefore extended to; Jim Lodwig Davies – Bath; Muriel and Leslie Davies – Moylgrove; Cecil Williams - St. Dogmaels; Barbara and the late David James – Shenfield; Desima Harris – Crymych; Nan Humphries – Llanfyllin; Roy Drury – Newcastle Emlyn; Sally Jones – London; Richard Jones – Australia; Margaret Evans – Cardigan; David Griffiths – Cardigan, and Dick Colman. I extend my thanks to Tony Bowen - St Dogmaels for taking the time to discuss with me the Maritime History of St Dogmaels and Cardigan, also to Glen Johnson - St Dogmaels for providing me with historical details of various St Dogmaels houses, and to Hugh Davies – Panteg, St Dogmaels for allowing me to view copies of the deeds to Panteg.

Finally I thank my niece Emma Helmke for sharing her IT skills with me.

Dedication

I dedicate this book to my very dear wife Rita. She has untiringly helped and encouraged me over the many years of research into my family tree. Together we have visited countless Record Offices in West Wales and London and she has endured, without complaint or protest, being dragged around so many graveyards, both kept and unkept, to find that elusive gravestone for each vital piece of information. To my Rita with much love and admiration.

CONTENTS

LIST OF ILLUSTRATIONS

Griffith David, son John Davies and his wife Mary

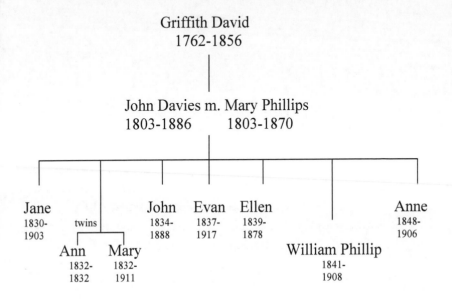

Griffith David
1762-1856

John Davies m. Mary Phillips
1803-1886   1803-1870

Jane   John   Evan   Ellen   Anne
1830-   twins 1834-   1837-   1839-   1848-
1903   1888   1917   1878   1906

    Ann   Mary   William Phillip
    1832- 1832-   1841-
    1832   1911   1908

CHAPTER 1

Griffith David, son John Davies and his wife Mary

In May 1803, after a brief truce, war resumed between Napoleon's France and Britain. It would be intriguing to know how much this event directly affected the people of Cardigan. It meant very little to the majority, I suspect. The same could be said I'm sure of another event that happened on the 2 July 1803, just a couple of months later, in the small parish of Ferwig just to the north of Cardigan. This was the birth of my great-great-grandfather John Davies.

His baptism was recorded in the Ferwig parish record for this year and it simply says 'John son of Griffith David baptized 13 July 1803'. John's father, Griffith David (his surname was later changed to Davies) was an agricultural labourer. I am uncertain of the name of John's mother because parish records etc. are scant for this period in some parishes, Ferwig being one of them. There are no records of any siblings that John might have had. Griffith was ninety-seven years old when he died in 1856, making his birth date about 1760. It is recorded in the Tremain parish records that a Griffith David was baptized there in 1762.

According to an electoral roll of 1813 Griffith Davies was living in a part of Capel Farm situated in the area around New Mill and Ty Newydd, just to the north of Cardigan. The first national census of 1841 records him as being an agricultural labourer living in part of New Mill itself. The 1851 census records him as a 92-year-old born in the parish of Tremain, residing in the same area in a house called Penpistill. This house does not exist today. It would be reasonable therefore to believe that Griffith had lived most of his life where the parishes of Ferwig, Tremain and St Mary's meet to the north of Cardigan and that John grew up here too. I have not found any evidence of John's education, if indeed he was formally educated. He certainly was able to read, write and navigate a ship later in his life.

For John, like hundreds of Cardigan men before and after him, the sea became an important part of his and his family's life. Cardigan's port, ship building industry and infrastructure were very busy at this time and were the lifeblood of Cardigan and the surrounding district; it was also a major employer. At one time Cardigan was one of the most important ports in Wales before the development of ports such as Newport, Cardiff and Swansea. Any product that could not be produced locally would have been brought in and distributed through its port. Among its exports were Cilgerran slate, salted herring, corn, butter, leather and tinplate from the tinplate works in Llechryd. Some of its imports were lime and culm[1] from Pembrokeshire, timber from the Baltics and North America, salt from Ireland, building material, general and luxury goods from Liverpool and Bristol.

John was apprenticed to John Davies, master of the ship *Active*, a Cardigan 'snow' (a two-masted ship with square sails) of 142 tons. He joined the ship on 20 January 1819 at the age of sixteen. The terms and length of an apprenticeship were usually set out in an indenture, which was signed by the child's parents or guardian and the master. The latter would promise to house, feed, clothe, and teach the apprentice a trade. The master received payment for this, usually paid by the child's father. If the child were a pauper the parish would arrange apprenticeships and pay the appropriate fee if it saw fit. Many apprenticeships were recorded in registers. Relatively few of these records survive today and I have been unable to locate John's.

On 11 April 1819 the *Active's* sister ship *Albion* left the port of Cardigan, the first ship to transport welsh emigrants directly from the Cardigan area to St. John's in Canada. The *Active* left Cardigan a few days later on almost the same itinerary, except she called in at Cork to pick up Irish emigrants for St. John's. It is believed that

---

1 Culm (cwlwm): anthracite dust mixed with clay, which made excellent fuel for domestic fires.

FOR

AMERICA.

THE FAST-SAILING BRIG,
CALLED THE

Active

~~Albion~~ *of Cardigan,*

~~John Llewellyn~~ DAVIES. MASTER,

Intends Sailing the beginning of next April, from
CARDIGAN with Passengers for SAINT JOHN'S
(NEW-BRUNSWICK) ~~and Newpitow.~~

For further Particulars (if by Letter Post-paid) enquire of Mr. John Davies,
Merchant, Cardigan, on or before the 28th of next February.

JANUARY 29 1820

AM

AMERICA.

Active Y LLONG HWYLUS,

~~ALBION~~ O ABERTEIFI,

CADPEN ~~Llewellyn~~ DAVIES,

Sydd yn bwriadu cludo Ymdeithwyr drosodd i
SAINT JOHN'S, BRUNSWICK-NEWYDD, ~~a Newpitow~~
~~Newpitow~~, ac i hwylio o ABERTEIFI tu a dechreu
Mis Ebrill nesaf.

Pawb ag sydd am gael eu trosglwyddo i un o'r Llefydd uchod, bydded
iddynt ddyfod at Mr. John Davies, Marsiandwr, i wneuthur cyttundeb am yr
arian cludi cyn diwedd Mis Chwefror nesaf.

ABERTEIFI, IONAWR 29 1820

JONATHAN HARRIS, PRINTER, DARK-GATE, CARMARTHEN.

John Davies would have been an apprentice on this voyage in 1820. *Courtesy of the National Library of Wales, Aberystwyth*

the *Albion* had been oversubscribed leaving some of her passengers behind. Subsequently the *Active* may also have had some of these emigrants on board.

On 30 June 1819 the *Active* arrived in the port of St John's, New Brunswick. On arrival they found the *Albion* already tied up in that port, having arrived just a few days earlier. After discharging their cargoes both ships loaded up with Canadian timber and set sail for home. The *Active* made similar voyages throughout 1820, 1821, and 1822. Young John as an apprentice on the *Active* would have gained valuable experience of sailing across the Atlantic very early in his career. Both vessels were owned by the entrepreneurial Davies family of Cardigan and Newport, Pembrokeshire. This family was so influential in the development of the port of Cardigan in the early nineteenth century.

The following is an extract taken from the diary of Dafydd Phillips, Baptist minister of Blaenwaun Chapel, St Dogmaels and a passenger on the following voyage.

"The Active's last voyage from St Johns in 1822: 28 June, set sail for Wales. Little progress was made during the first few days due to very light winds and they were still in the Bay of Fundy on the 3 July. In the afternoon of the 5 July the Captain, myself and two apprentices boarded an American fishing smack where we obtained salt and fresh Cod in exchange for a piece of pork and a bottle of rum"

John could well have been one of the two apprentices that boarded the fishing smack.

He went on to make a life long career at sea and later became a mate and master with financial interests in at least three ships. In 1850 it became compulsory for masters and mates of ships to take examinations to test their seafaring skills. The men who passed were given Certificates of Service. John was examined to become a master mariner in the port of Liverpool in December 1850. Both his certificate and the application he made to be examined survive. They both hold a large amount of information about him: date of birth, address at the time, service number and an account of all his previous experience at sea, i.e. ships served on, dates of joining and leaving, ranks held, whether foreign or coasting trade, size and home port of ships served thus far in his career.

These were two most valuable documents to discover. They recorded more than thirty years of John Davies' career in one fell

John Davies' Master's Certificate of Service issued at the Port of Liverpool in December 1850.
Courtesy of the National Archives, Kew

swoop. I have subsequently found a contradiction in some of the dates provided in the above application which I will explain later. His address in 1850 was Panteg, St Dogmaels.

On the 15 October 1822 John's service on the _Active_ terminated but he was soon back at sea. The following is a list of the other ships that John served on from 15 October 1822 until the end of 1823, giving the vessels' names, date of signing on, position held, home port, tonnage and whether coastal or foreign trading:

Ship	Port of Reg.	Tons	Position held	From	Trade
Mary Ann	Aberystwyth	55	Seaman	Oct 1822	Coastal
Elizabeth	Liverpool	260	Seaman	March 1823	Foreign
Higginson	Liverpool	400	Seaman	March 1823	Foreign
Hotspur	Workington	170	Seaman	May 1823	Foreign

Twenty-year-old John was fast becoming an experienced sailor. Prior to 1823 he had been employed on five different ships, signing off the _Hotspur_ on 15 December. But 1823 was not over just yet. The very next day he was off on another new venture, one that deserves a few paragraphs of its own.

5

In his application to be examined as master in 1850 it is recorded that on 16 December 1823 he joined the fifty-gun Ship HMS *Romney* in Quebec, Canada. The *Romney*, a fourth rater[2], was under the command of Capt. N Lockyard and even though she was classed as a fifty-gun ship she only had thirty guns. She was never involved in any sea battles while John was a member of her crew but was used almost exclusively by the Royal Navy as a troop carrier. On this particular voyage she was transporting the principle division of the Seventy Ninth Regiment of Cameron Highlanders. The navy had many troop ships and their roll was to transport soldiers and officials across the sea to allow Britain to keep a firm hold of her Empire. The arrival of the *Romney* in Quebec was much celebrated, as an article published in the Montréal Mercury on the 1 November 1825 indicates:

> *"We are much gratified in announcing the safe arrival yesterday of his Majesty's Ship, Captain Lockyard, CB and the transporter 'Maria', with the remaining division of the 79th Regiment; for the safety of which apprehension began to be entertained. In the course of this morning the Headquarters Division, under Colonel Douglas, disembarked from HMS the companies under Major Campbell from the 'Maria', having landed yesterday and marched into the Jesuit's Barracks.... But whilst hailing the arrival of the gallant strangers, we must not lose sight of our old friends, the 37th Regiment, who are about to take their departure in the vessels which brought the Cameron Highlanders...."*

The *Romney's* muster rolls however show that John did not join the ship on the above date as it states on his application to become master but instead two years later on 2 November 1825. He joined as a volunteer and was not press-ganged in to service. When considering this discrepancy the first question is, what happened to John during these two unaccounted for years? Why and what was his business in Quebec (he had previously been to Canada whilst serving on the *Active*)? Had he been in Canada since his discharge from the *Hotspur*

2 In the British Royal Navy, a fourth-rate was, during the first half of the 18th century, a ship of the line mounting from 46 up to 60 guns.

in December 1823? The reason for the discrepancy is probably quite simple. While completing his application form in Liverpool in 1850, twenty-six years later, he may have forgotten the exact dates he left and joined those ships all that time before and simply, in an attempt to make the form coherent and tidy, did the best he could. The records of arrivals and departures of ships at the port of Quebec for 1825 lend support to this theory. They show that the above ship *Hotspur* did arrive in that port on 11 October from Liverpool with a cargo of salt. They had set out from Liverpool on the 20 August some fifty days or so earlier, quite a slow crossing even for those days. The *Hotspur* stayed in port, discharging her cargo, and began her return journey to Liverpool on 3 November. John was most certainly a member of her crew when she arrived but was not on the return leg of the voyage for he had volunteered to join HMS *Romney* on 2 November, the day before the *Hotspur's* departure.

John was employed as an able seaman on the *Romney* and every able seaman in the Royal Navy in those days would have needed at least two years experience at sea. An able seaman's work in the main were carried out on the top deck of a ship, consisting of such duties as helming the ship, aloft trimming and maintaining the rigging, lookout duties and the using of the lead etc. By now John was well qualified and had become a seasoned sailor on large vessels and Atlantic crossings, but what was he to make of the rigorous discipline on board Royal Navy ships?

On 13 April 1826 at 11.00 hours the ship's company were mustered to witness punishments doled out. Seaman J Whitton was given twenty-four lashes for drunkenness, Thomas Cousins twenty-four lashes for neglect of duty and disobedience of orders, William Kelsey twenty-one lashes for being off deck on his watch and Edward Jones twelve lashes for drunkenness and spitting. John would have witnessed these punishments possibly for the first time in his life.

By 26 May the *Romney* had returned home and was at anchor in Plymouth Sound. She proved to be a busy ship during the two years or so of John's service. Her duties took her and John to and from the Mediterranean and the ports of Gibraltar, Malta and Lisbon. On 7 August 1827 the *Romney* again returned to the St Laurence

River, anchoring in the port of Quebec on the twelfth. This time she transported 400 men of the Sixty-Sixth Regiment to that colony and was again back at sea on the twenty-eighth of the month. After a swift crossing of the Atlantic she was anchored in Plymouth Sound by 21 September.

This was the last voyage John was to make on HMS *Romney* for he was 'paid off' on 18 October 1827. This date of discharge is confirmed by the date provided on the *Romney's* muster roles, but again contradicts the date John supplies on the application form mentioned previously, which was 20 September 1826, one whole year earlier. Whatever the detail, he would have had the experience of a lifetime as a sailor in the Royal Navy and, whether it was good or bad, he would have become a better and wiser man because of it.

Points of interest from Quebec:

"On Sunday, being the 5th November 1825, the anniversary of the discovery of the famous plot in 1605, the 'Romney', Captain, Lockyard, fired the usual royal salute." Quebec Mercury

"Amongst the late arrival of the brig 'Agenoria', from Aberystwyth, on board which came 15 welsh settlers, their singular costumes and dialect rendered them objects of much curiosity. The Welsh are in general a hardy and industrious race and we should be happy in seeing further importations of them. As with these qualifications they promise to make steady and useful settlers." Quebec Mercury

After his discharge John made his way to Swansea and joined the 120-ton coaster *Hope*. On this vessel he was employed as the ship's mate. His confidence in his own ability and judgment must have been growing, to take on such a responsibility. After all, the mate takes the helm if anything happens to the master. He sailed on the *Hope* until 4 March 1828 after which he returned home to Cardigan and I dare say to a very warm welcome from his father. He became the mate of the Cardigan registered coaster *Wellington* a sloop of some 55 tons. Small coasters such as this would have had very few crewmembers, three or four men at the most. He remained her mate until June 1831.

Perhaps John's father was not the only person to welcome him home, for he had met, or was soon to meet, the young lady who was to become his wife. On the 24 March 1829 in St Mary's Church Cardigan John married Mary Phillips of this parish, in the presence of Evan and William Phillips (probably members of Mary's family). John signed the register and Mary made her mark. Her mother's name was also Mary and her father was Rhoderick, another of Cardigan's many mariners. At first they made their home in the Bridge End area of Cardigan and it wasn't long before they started a family. Their first daughter Jane was born on 2 January 1830 and baptized in Capel Mair, Cardigan.

John was still hard at work and had eyes on bigger and better things, for on 1 December 1831 he was registered as mate of the 60 ton Cardigan schooner *Thetis*. Just five days later on the sixth he was registered as her master, also on that day he bought four of the *Thetis'* sixty-four shares from a Benjamin James of Cardigan. Not only would he now be paid for his work but also share in any profits the ship made. For the remainder of her life, the *Thetis* was registered as a coaster and traded along the coasts of Great Britain and Ireland.

It was not unusual then for masters to purchase a number of shares in their own vessels as it was for all manner of individuals. Merchants, farmers, tradesmen, clergymen, squires, widows, and schoolmasters were commonly listed as shareholders in registration books of ships in those days. The registration book of the port of Cardigan shows that there were nine individuals holding the total of sixty-four shares in the *Thetis* in 1836. Of these two were mariners, two merchants, three widows, a spinster and a gentleman. One of the co-owners was usually chosen to be the managing owner, who had the authority to do all that was necessary to make sure the ship sailed and delivered cargo, often using agents to do this. The master himself quite often took on this responsibility, but any other shareholder could be appointed.

Mary was very much pregnant again by early 1832 giving birth to twins on 3 April. Their names were Mary and Anne. Unfortunately Anne died in infancy. Mary was later to marry a master mariner.

The twins were baptized on 10 June, also in Capel Mair. Two years went by before the birth of their first son on 25 October 1834. He was named John like his father and also like his father was to become a master mariner, part owner and shareholder of a ship. Like his sisters John was baptized in Capel Mair.

A Fine Family Home

Things were going well for John in both his family and business life, for the deeds of the house show that in May 1835 he bought Panteg, a large house situated on the left hand side as you enter St Dogmaels from Cardigan. The deeds say that John Davies, of Bridge End Cardigan bought Panteg formally known as Mwtchwr from David Mendis, a carpenter of St Dogmaels, for the sum of £43. Panteg was a fairly substantial house with a good size garden and orchard. John and Mary must have been proud of themselves when they made this purchase. They were certainly on the way up from John's humble beginnings. By 1840 Mary had given birth to two more children. Evan, born on 9 July 1837, followed in his father's footsteps and became a master mariner. Ellen, born in 1839, later married an Aberporth master mariner. John was surely a happy man at this time for it seemed that there was much contentment at home

Panteg circa. 1870

10

and success in his business.

Life for Cardiganshire mariners has always been a harsh and perilous one. The wind on this coast was notorious for its frequent and sudden change in direction and speed, reaching gale force in minutes, with treacherous currents and underwater rocks adding to the dangerous hazards that faced mariners of long ago. It was thought at the time that there were ten vessels lost on the welsh coast as opposed to one on the Irish side of St Georges channel. Thomas Jones, vicar of St Dogmaels noted the following in the parish register in 1789:

"Early one morning some fishermen in their boats were lying under shelter between Little Quay and Allt y Coed waiting for the tide to turn to take them back onto the River Tivy when suddenly, the wind changed direction and increased to gale force creating 'tempestuous conditions', the sea 'carrying all before it'. Some of the fishing boats were washed onto the rocks and others onto the beach. In all, 27 men were 'swallowed up by the angry elements'."

The deeds of Panteg together with the 'Port of Cardigan Register' referring to the ship *Thetis* gives us a wonderful opportunity to look at John's business and financial life in the 1840s to the 1870s. The following is just a brief glimpse at that part of his life during that time. For reasons not known, in March 1840 John borrowed £100 from Elizabeth James, a widow, of Park y Prat, St Dogmaels; Panteg was used as security for the loan.

Banks and Building Societies were not as available then as they are today of course and personal borrowing of money was a more common method of acquiring credit. It was also a profitable proposition for the lender, as 5 per cent or so interest was often charged, as in this case. One possible reason for this loan was to acquire further shares in his ship *Thetis*. On 6 September of this year Elizabeth Ann Bowen transferred twelve shares by Bill of Sale to John Davies, and this year was also the first year it was recorded in the Lloyds Register of Shipping that the owners of the *Thetis* were John Davies & Co. John's business was now a registered company.

The Lloyds Registers covering the years 1836 to 1850 give a brief description of the *Thetis'* trading patterns. For the first four years she was on a London to Newry run and subsequent years she was a Cork Coaster, Liverpool Coaster, London Coaster and for the last four a Cardiff Coaster, so it seemed that John and the *Thetis* sailed very few voyages out of their home port of Cardigan. Coasters were a vital and important method for transporting goods from place to place especially before the introduction of the railway networks.

Matters of Interest

An Indenture dated 23 February 1843 states that the above-mentioned Elizabeth James, widow of Park y Prat, St Dogmaels had subsequently remarried to Rev. John Jones (Methodist Minister of Blaenanerch Chapel) of Rhosygadir in the parish of Tremain. Elizabeth and her new husband requested the return of the £100 lent to John Davies in March of 1840, plus interest. As it was not convenient for John to pay at this time, he asked John Davies of Troedyraur in the County of Cardigan to pay on his behalf and also asked for a further loan of £150 for himself. This made a total of £250 pounds borrowed by John Davies of Panteg from John Davies of Troedyraur, a quite substantial sum at that time.

The rate of interest was 5 per cent per annum and it was agreed that the money borrowed would be paid back by the following February. Panteg and two recently built houses in the grounds of Panteg were used as security for this loan. The fact that the two houses recently erected in the grounds of Panteg were included as part security for the loan indicates that John owned the two properties. As they were recently built it could also be considered that John had them built for himself. There is a photograph of Panteg taken circa. 1870 which shows a cottage attached to each gable end.

Also on 27 February of this year John acquired by Bill of Sale from David Davies, a Merchant of Cardigan sixteen more shares in his ship *Thetis* and peculiarly, on 5 December also of this year, John transfers back to David Davies of the Castle, Cardigan the same sixteen shares.

In January 1847 John Davies asked Matilda and Elinor Makeig[3],

3 The 1844 Pigot's Trade Directory of South Wales describes Matilda and Elinor Makeig as Spirit and Wine Merchants, High Street, Cardigan

both spinsters of Cardigan Town to lend him £150 so he could pay back that amount to John Davies of Troedyraur. This they agreed to do. The conditions of this loan seemed to be the same as the others. Panteg was again used as security and an annual rate of interest of 5 per cent was paid. A year later John, on 15 December 1848, purchased by Bill of Sale four *Thetis* shares from Thomas Griffith of Cardigan. This made a total of twenty shares owned by John, practically a third of the total of the *Thetis*' sixty-four.

The following is an entry made in the deeds of Panteg in April 1863 and is probably best understood by reading it in its entirety:

> *"I the undersigned James Thomas Makeig James the executor of the last will and testament of George Makeig who was the executor of the last will and testament of the within named Elinor Makeig hereby acknowledge that I have this day received of the written named John Davies of Panteg the within mentioned One Hundred and Fifty pounds and all interest due therein. As witness my hand this twenty-ninth day of April One thousand Eight Hundred and Sixty Three."*

It was signed James Thomas Makeig James. The two Makeig sisters had obviously died, as had the executor of Elinor's will George Makeig. James, George's nephew, was tidying up his uncle's affairs and rightly retrieving any outstanding debts. As for John Davies, in the eighteen thirties and forties he seems to have had a keen eye for business, as he had borrowed and invested money well. Investors were confident enough not only to invest in him but also to lend him money. He seemed confident in himself as a businessman and master mariner, making good use of his beloved schooner *Thetis*.

Two years later on 16 January 1865 John and his wife Mary made a statutory declaration to state that they were in actual possession of the house and lands purchased in 1835, meaning Panteg. This is because they intended to sell the premises to Richard Lloyd, a sale from which they made a very substantial profit, selling the premises for £900 when they only paid £43 just thirty years earlier. This was an excellent deal in anyone's book.

Panteg - A Full House

What about their family life in Panteg? The first National Census Record was taken in June 1841 and it shows that John and Mary were living in Panteg with their children. Also living there were Mary's forty-year-old brother Evan and her eighty-year-old widowed mother also called Mary. They also employed twenty-year-old Margaret Evans as a maid. John was not recorded in this census probably because he was at sea. The following is a list of occupants.

Place	Name	Age	Profession/Status
Panteg	Mary Phillips4	80	Widow
	Evan Phillips	40	Mariner
	Mary Davies	35	Master Mariner's wife
	Jane Davies	11	
	Mary Davies	9	
	John Davies	7	
	Evan Davies	4	
	Eleanor Davies (Ellen)	2	
	Margaret Evans	20	Maid

Sometime after the census was taken in 1841 John and Mary's seventh child was born. His name was William Phillip. He also became a master mariner in later life.

In 1848 Mary gave birth to the last of her eight children. She was another girl and was given the name Anne, perhaps in remembrance of the sister born in 1832 who had died in infancy.

The 1851 census shows John at home with his wife and family. Two of the children were not there: seventeen-year-old Mary had married a mariner named William Evans from Aberaeron in June 1850 and was living in one of the cottages attached to Panteg, and twenty-two-year-old Jane had married David Evans a ship's carpenter

---

4 Eighty-year-old Mary Phillips, widow of Rhoderick, died of old age on 4 June 1845. She had spent the last few years of her life being looked after by her daughter Mary and son-in-law John Davies in Panteg. She was buried in St Mary's Parish Church grave-yard, Cardigan. After many hours of looking for her gravestone I have found no trace of it.

No. of Schedule	Parish or Township of St. Dogmaels	Ecclesiastical District of St. Dogmaels	City or Borough of Cardigan	Town of	Village of	Name of Street, Place, or Road, and Name or No. of House	Name and Surname of each Person who abode in the house, on the Night of the 30th March, 1851	Relation to Head of Family	Condition	Age of Males	Age of Females	Rank, Profession, or Occupation	Where Born	Whether Blind, or Deaf-and-Dumb
1						Cadipon Lane (Panty)	John Davies	Head	Married	40		Baker Mariner	St Dogmaels Parish	
							Mary Davies	Wife	Married		36	Bo - Wife	do	
							John Davies	Son	Unmarried	16		Seaman	do	
							Lewis Davies	Son		14		do	do	
							William Davies	Son		9		Scholar	do	
							Anna Davies	Daughter			7	do	do	
							Hannah Phillips	Servant			13	House maid	do	
2						Cadipon Lane	Mary Lucas	Head	Widow		70	Mariner's Wife	St Dogmaels Parish	

Total of Houses: 1 2 U 1 B —
Total of Persons.. 4 5

The above is a copy of the 1851 Census return for Panteg, St Dogmaels

15

from New Quay in December 1851. Below are the remaining family members living in Panteg at this time.

Name	Relationship	Marriage	Age	Profession
John Davies	Head	Married	49	Master Mariner
Mary Davies	Wife	Married	48	Master Mariners Wife
John Davies	Son	Un-married	16	Seaman
Evan Davies	Son	Un-married	14	Seaman
Ellen Davies	Daughter	Un-married	11	Scholar
William Davies	Son	Un-married	9	Scholar
Ann Davies	Daughter	Un-married	3	Scholar
Hannah Phillips	Maid	Un-married	17	House Maid

It is interesting to note that the two eldest sons John and Evan had already become seamen like their father. Young Evan began his seafaring career as an apprentice on his father's ship the *Thetis* in 1849 at just twelve years old. The children were growing up fast.

The 1850s was a relatively less uneventful decade for the Davies' of Panteg. However there were two significant occurrences. The first was the death of John Davies' father, Griffith Davies. At the time of his death he was living with his son John and daughter-in-law Mary in Panteg. On his death certificate it says that he died on 5 February 1856 at Panteg, a ninety-seven-year-old agricultural labourer. The cause of death was old age. His son John registered the death in Cardigan the very next day. He was buried in the parish church of Ferwig. Again, after a long and careful search of this graveyard, I was unable to locate his gravestone. If he had, which seems likely, been an agricultural labourer all of his life, he lived to a ripe old age considering the difficult time in which he lived, the demands and hard work of his occupation and the wet West Wales climate. It's a nice thought to know that his son and daughter-in-law looked after him in Panteg for the last days of his life.

The second significant occurrence was the marriage of John and Mary's eldest son John to Frances Lodwig of Pantywylan Farm, Moylgrove on 6 September 1859. They were both twenty-five years old. Frances' parents were Benjamin and Leah Lodwig. Benjamin was also a master mariner with financial interests in Cardigan ships. This was the bringing together of two seafaring families who understood the business, the harshness of this life, the long separations, trading of their cargos and even the buying and selling of their ships. This marriage was a pretty good match.

In 1861 another National Census was taken. Of the seven surviving Panteg children, five had flown the nest leaving just two at home. The following is a list of occupants living there when the census was taken.

Name	Relationship	Marriage	Age	Profession
John Davies	Head	Married	58	Seaman
Mary Davies	Wife	Married	58	Seaman's wife
William Davies	Son	Un-married	20	Seaman
Anne Davies	Daughter	Un-married	14	Scholar

The above is an abbreviated copy of the 1861 Census return for Panteg, St Dogmaels (The enumerator on this occasion records John as a seaman but he was and had been an established Master Mariner for thirty years at this time. See 1851 census return above).

Mary, the second eldest of the children was, as in 1851, living in one of the cottages that were attached to Panteg. She was listed as a twenty-nine-year-old seaman's wife. Ellen was visiting her eldest married sister Jane and family in Barry Island, Glamorganshire. William, the youngest of the three Panteg sons, had now become a seaman. There was truly much salt water running through the veins of this particular Davies family.

1863 was a busy year for John and the *Thetis* as the document 'Account of Voyages and Crew' records. This document had to be completed by every ship's master twice a year and handed to the Shipping Master at a vessel's Registered Home Port on July 1 and 31 December or at the earliest possible time after that. For the first half of this year John was her Managing Owner, for the remaining six months David Davies of Castle Green Cardigan was the Managing Owner. John was also her master and Benjamin Jones was mate. There were also two able seamen and one apprentice on board, all from St Dogmaels. The apprentice was fifteen-year-old John Thomas. During the course of the year a total of fifteen voyages were made to ten destinations.

The vessel was laid up in Cardigan until 15 March, probably waiting for the worst of the winter weather to be over before commencing her trading for the year. The destinations were: the ports of Cardiff and Waterford three times each, Cork, Liverpool, Gloucester, Fiddown (near Waterford), Port Talbot, Newport, and Balenacorow. The *Thetis* returned to Cardigan on 9 December of the same year and was probably tied up on the river Tivy for the remainder of the winter.

There were no details of cargoes given on these documents but we do know that the South Wales ports of Newport and Cardiff were extremely busy with coal exporting, as was Port Talbot, with steel and tinplate works. Swansea was well known not only for its coal exports but also for copper smelting, steel, iron and tinplate works. The *Thetis'* cargoes would almost certainly have been some of these commodities.

As mentioned earlier, in January 1865 John and Mary made a statutory declaration regarding Panteg in preparation to sell the house to Richard Lloyd. They were still living there on 28 March 1865, because Panteg was the address on the marriage certificate of their twenty-six-year- old daughter Ellen when she married George Owens, a master mariner of the White Lion, Aberporth. Soon afterwards John and Mary moved from Panteg into the 'Sailors Home,' a Public House in St. Dogmaels, when John became its landlord.

This public house does not exist today. It stood on the spot where there is now a little public garden called Halket Square on the junction of Graig Terrace and High Street. In 1865 when John was approaching his sixty-third birthday, were his thoughts turning slowly towards retirement, as by January 1866 he had sold the *Thetis*?

The new owner was E H Davies of Union Street, Carmarthen. Unfortunately, on 30 November of that year this little vessel met her end. She was lost whilst on a voyage from Carmarthen to Greenock. Miraculously her master and all her crew were saved. Even though he was not now her owner or master and that all the crew had been saved John must have been a little sad when he heard of the loss. He himself had sailed on her as master, and John Davies & Co had been her official owners for over thirty years. She must have been close to his heart.

However, John Davies & Co about this time purchased another ship, a 35-ton smack (a small single-masted vessel mainly used for coastal voyages) by the name of *Ellen Owens*. This little ship had been built in 1861 on the banks of the River Tivy practically across the river from Panteg and the village of St Dogmaels.

John's youngest son William became her master and John himself her managing owner. From 1 July to 13 December of that year the *Ellen Owens* made eight consecutive voyages between Cardigan and Bristol. William remained the master of this ship until the mid 1890s.

The year of 1870 was the very saddest of years for the Davies family of Panteg, for sixty-seven-year-old Mary, dear wife of John and mother to their eight children, died of bronchitis on 7 August. They had been married for forty-one years. She had been twenty-six years old when they married in 1829 and gave birth to their first child Jane the following year. She was forty-five years old when their last child Ann was born in 1848.

They had been through a lot of ups and downs together as families always do, yet this must have been a mighty blow to everyone. John, who was the same age as his wife, had retired by this time for he was described as a retired master mariner on Mary's death certificate; their address was the 'Sailors Home' public house, St Dogmaels. Mary was buried in St Dogmaels Parish Church graveyard.

The following year, as the 1871 census records, John was still the landlord of 'Sailors Home' and living with him as house helper was his seventeen-year-old granddaughter Mary Anne Evans (his daughter Jane's eldest child). John was forging himself a new career, for his occupation as recorded in this census was 'fisherman'. It is known from his Last Will and Testament that he was in possession of herring nets. During the taking of this very census *Ellen Owens* was recorded tied up in the harbour of Portmadoc with a total of three

19

Memorial Stone of John and Mary Davies

crew members on board. The master was his son William Davies, the crew one mate and one boy. All were from St Dogmaels. They were probably loading a cargo of roofing slates that were quarried in the hills above that town.

Ten years later, in 1881 *Ellen Owens* was in the port of Swansea with William remaining as her master and again with a mate and a boy. The *Ellen Owens* certainly was a busy little vessel.

John wrote his Last Will and Testament in April 1879. He was still the landlord of the 'Sailors Home' and he appointed his son William and his son in law Lewis Davies of Penrallt-y-dre as trustees and executors of his will. He remained in the 'Sailors Home' until at least the date that the 1881 census was taken as he is recorded living there with his granddaughter, twelve-year-old Mary Ellen Owens. He employed a Jane Evans as general servant.

Soon after the census John moved out of the 'Sailors Home' and into a house situated just a few yards down the High Street called Britannia House. It was in this house that on 30 July 1886 John died. According to the Burial Records of St Dogmaels Parish Church of St. Thomas, he was buried there on 3 August. A short obituary appeared in The Cardigan and Tivyside Advertiser the following week. It read as follows:

"DAVIES-On 30th Ultimo, at High St. St Dogmaels, Captain John Davies formerly of the Sailors Home Inn, aged 84 years. Much respected."

On the first day of September, one month later, probate of his Will was granted to William and Lewis the executors and administrators.

John was short of his father's age at death by twelve years but even so, eighty-four years must be considered a very good innings indeed and looking back over his life I think he would have been pleased with his achievements. He started out with little, went to sea as a young man, had many adventures, married a good woman and had a good size family. He was very entrepreneurial in his business and had a long life in which to enjoy it too. It could certainly be said he was a kind and good person, especially to his family.

He encouraged his three sons to follow in his footsteps and take up a career at sea. Two of them were apprentices on his ship *Thetis* and one sailed his vessel *Ellen Owens*. All three became exemplary master mariners in their own right. Three of his four surviving daughters married into families with seafaring connections. He also showed his caring side as he considered his late daughter Ellen's two children in his will. He instructs his trustees to invest their mother's share of the inheritance and use it towards their welfare. He was certainly a true family man.

The following is John's Will in its entirety:

"This is the last Will and Testament of me John Davies of the "Sailors Home" in the village of St. Dogmaels in the county of Pembroke, retired Master Mariner. After paying all my just debts funeral and testamentary expenses I give and bequeath immediately after my decease my Smack 'Ellen Owen' with all the gear and tackle thereto belonging also my herring nets unto my son William absolutely. All the residue of my property real and personal I give devise and bequeath unto my trustees hereafter named their heirs executors administrators and assigns upon trust as soon as conveniently might be after my decease to convert into money and as to the proceeds thereafter to divide the sum between all my children share and share alike and I direct that the children of my late daughter Ellen to take their mothers share equally but in case one of them shall happen to die before attaining the age of twenty one years without leaving lawful issue his or her share shall go to other of them absolutely. And I direct my said trustees to invest the same to the best advantage in case if need be to be applied towards their maintenance and education. I appoint my said son William and my son in law Lewis Davies trustees and executors of this my will. And I declare that my said trustees shall not be answerable for involuntary losses nor be accountable for any other than wilful acts or negligence and that it shall be lawful for them to reimburse themselves of all expenses they might be put to and expend on the execution of this trust of my will. In witness whereof I hereunto set my hand this 25th day of April 1879---John Davies---Signed by the testator John Davies as his last will and testament in the presence of us being present at the same time who at his request in his presence and in the presence of each other inscribe our names as witnesses--- J.M.Davies Independent Minister---James James, Maltser."

John's family, with all its involvement with the sea, were by no means unique in St Dogmaels in those days. The sea was the lifeblood of the village; its mariners were well known and respected by ship owners in all of the most important ports of Great Britain. St Dogmaels also possessed a busy fishing industry and therefore was very heavily populated by mariners and fishermen alike. They sailed from there to the four corners of the world.

Jane, John and Mary Davies' first child

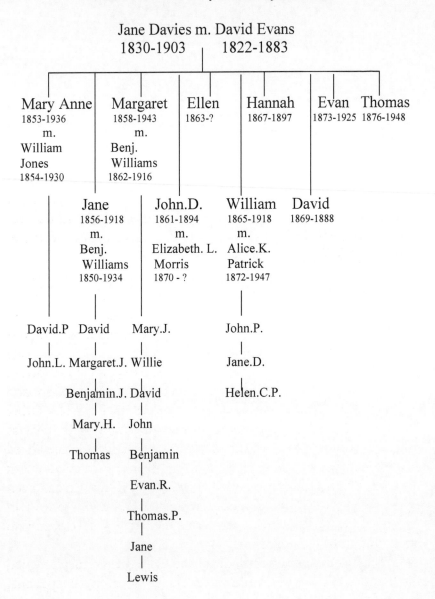

Jane Davies m. David Evans
1830-1903   1822-1883

Mary Anne	Margaret	Ellen	Hannah	Evan	Thomas
1853-1936	1858-1943	1863-?	1867-1897	1873-1925	1876-1948
m.	m.				
William	Benj.				
Jones	Williams				
1854-1930	1862-1916				

Jane	John.D.	William	David
1856-1918	1861-1894	1865-1918	1869-1888
m.	m.	m.	
Benj.	Elizabeth. L.	Alice.K.	
Williams	Morris	Patrick	
1850-1934	1870 - ?	1872-1947	

David.P   David   Mary.J.   John.P.

John.L. Margaret.J. Willie   Jane.D.

Benjamin.J. David   Helen.C.P.

Mary.H.   John

Thomas   Benjamin

Evan.R.

Thomas.P.

Jane

Lewis

24

CHAPTER 2

Jane – John and Mary Davies' first child

Jane was the first of John and Mary's children, born on 2 January 1830. The family was living in Cardigan at this time, in the area known as Bridge End. In 1835 they moved to live in Panteg, St Dogmaels where Jane spent her formative years. In the 1841 census she was recorded as an eleven-year-old girl living with her family. It is not known if Jane received a formal education. If she did, it might have been at the 'National School' in the village. This school was founded by the Church of England and Church of Wales and was in existence in St Dogmaels at this time.

By 1851 she had met her future husband and they married on 9 December of that year. Just like her mother she went on to have a large family, but unlike her mother did not marry a mariner. Even so the sea was to feature a great deal in her family's life. Her husband was David Evans and the information given on the marriage certificate states that David was a twenty-nine-year-old bachelor who resided in Cardigan, his occupation being a carpenter. (In all later information regarding David he is recorded as a ship's carpenter). His father was William Evans, a shipwright. This particular Evans family was originally from New Quay. According to census records they lived at No 5 Penygeulan, New Quay. David, I suspect had been taught his trade by his father in New Quay, where shipbuilding had been established for many decades, and had come to Cardigan to work in its busy shipbuilding yards. Both towns had by now developed into strong maritime communities.

It is probably safe to say that Jane and David began their married life living with her parents at Panteg. Their first child, Mary Anne, was born there in November 1853. Jane, their second daughter was born in 1856 followed by Margaret in December 1858. It is indicated on later census returns that the latter of the two daughters was born in Cardigan. Maybe Jane and David had at some time moved out of Panteg and into a home of their own in Cardigan.

By 1861 Jane, David and their three daughters had moved to Barry Island to live. Their fourth child, a son, was born there in the spring of that year. His name was John Davies Evans. What attracted them to this quiet little hamlet? Barry Island in 1861 had only two houses in total and approximately twenty-one inhabitants living in them. Five of the inhabitants were lodgers in Jane and David's house; two of these were ship's carpenters, one from Cardigan and one from New Quay, and the third a blacksmith, also from Cardigan.

Bustling Barry Town

Barry Town, with its primitive harbour, could boast less than one hundred inhabitants and amongst these, lodging in a public house called 'The Ship' were two other ship's carpenters and a blacksmith, all from New Quay. Barry at that time was twenty years or so away from developing into one of the largest coal exporting ports in South Wales[1]. On the other hand its neighbour Cardiff, situated just seven miles or so to the east, was already well on its way to becoming the massive coal exporting port of the late nineteenth and early twentieth centuries. For David and his peers the rapid development of Cardiff meant a corresponding need for shipwrights, ship's carpenters and ancillary trades such as anchor makers, block makers, sail makers and rope makers. This alone would surely be the attraction to bring tradesmen like David from their West Wales coastal villages and towns. If the shipbuilding industry in Cardigan and New Quay were busy, the port of Cardiff was in a different league.

It doesn't seem that David, Jane and family lived in Barry Island,

---

1 Barry docks, just like its neighbour, was developed specifically to export coal from the South Wales valleys. It grew very rapidly, exporting from about one million tons during its first year of operation in 1889, to a massive twelve to thirteen million tons in 1914. Pit props were a large proportion of its imports as of course the coal mines of the Glamorgan Valleys needed an endless supply of them. Canada, Norway, and the Baltic countries traditionally were the suppliers for the British market.

Glamorganshire for many years, because by the 1871 census Jane had given birth to four more children, all of them born in New Quay. There was Ellen in 1863, William in 1865, Hannah in 1867, and David in 1869. The census returns for that year also reveal an odd phenomenon. It shows that David and Jane were boarders at 1 William Street, Cardiff. This was the house of New Quay sail maker James James and his family. Yet seven of their children were living at 18 Park Street, New Quay. Their fifteen-year-old daughter Jane was recorded as the housekeeper, presumably looking after her younger siblings.

What possible explanation could there be for the parents to be living apart from their children? Did David, perhaps with a pang of 'hiraeth'[2] in his heart for his beloved New Quay, decide to move his family back there while he stayed on in Cardiff a little longer making a good living and was Jane perhaps visiting her husband on that census taking day?

In the 1881 census David and Jane are shown to have moved to 20 Mariners Row (later to become Marine Terrace), New Quay. This house was to remain in the family's hands for at least the next forty years. Two other children had been born there: Evan in 1873 and Thomas in 1875. David was recorded as a fifty-nine-year-old ship's carpenter, whether he still worked or not is unknown. The ship building industry in New Quay had declined somewhat by the 1880s. The children that were still living at home in 1881 were Hannah, David, Evan, and Thomas.

Sadly, Jane became a widow when David died on 4 February 1883. He was buried in the Parish Church of Llanllwchaiarn (New Quay). David had been a ship's carpenter for almost all of his life and would have had a wealth of experience building and repairing wooden ships. He had worked in New Quay, Cardigan, and Cardiff, all of which had extremely busy shipyards.

The building of wooden ships declined rapidly towards the end of the nineteenth century. The reason was simply the introduction of steam ships. Steam engines had become far more reliable; they didn't have to rely on the wind and tide and the ships themselves, being built of steel could be made much bigger and carry much

2 'hiraeth' is a Welsh word for a nostalgic longing or to yearn.

larger cargoes, giving them a huge advantage over their sailing counterparts.

The death of her husband was not the only tragedy to befall Jane in the 1880s. Her son David died at sea whilst serving as an ordinary seaman on a ship called *Ryevale*. At the time of his death this ship was at sea and he was quite likely to have been given a sea burial. He is remembered on his father's gravestone with the simple words:

'David, bu farw ar y mor Hyd. 11, 1888 yn 20 oed'. (David died at sea on October 11th 1888 at 20 years of age).'

Jane was still living at 20 Mariners Terrace when the 1891 census was taken. She was described as a sixty-one-year-old widow living on her own means. Also living with her was her son Thomas who was employed as an apprentice tailor and her nine-year-old grandson David S Evans.

Jane suffered bereavement twice more in the 1890s when another two of her children died. The first was her eldest son John Davies Evans. Like his brother David, John died at sea whilst serving as master of the ship *Ullock* on 29 January 1894. Seafaring was certainly a perilous occupation in those days. Whole families would have been affected when these disasters befell them, especially the mothers and wives, and John had both. Jane's daughter Hannah died three years later on the 29 March 1897. Both these children's deaths are recorded on their father's gravestone at New Quay.

Jane remained living at 20 Mariners Terrace until her death on 17 November 1903. She was seventy-three years old when she died. She had given birth to ten children over a period of three decades and had outlived four of them. The sea had certainly featured in Jane's life, as not only were her father and brothers mariners, but her husband had made a living from it, two of her sons had perished on it and each community she lived in had the sea in their souls. Jane was buried with her husband in New Quay.

Jane and David Evans' children

Mary Anne was the first of Jane and David's children. She was born in St Dogmaels on the 24 November 1853 and by 1861 she was, naturally, living with her parents in Barry Island. When she was about seventeen years old she had moved back to live with her grandfather John Davies in High Street, St Dogmaels. John had been widowed two years earlier and I suspect Mary Anne was pleasant company for the old man. She was recorded as his house helper in that year's census return.

In 1874 Mary Anne followed what was becoming something of a tradition for many of the women in this family, which was to marry a mariner or at least someone connected with the sea. Mary Anne's choice was William Jones from Newport, Pembrokeshire and his occupation, as recorded on the marriage certificate, was a mariner. William's father Peter was also a mariner. They were married in the parish church of Llanllwchaiarn (New Quay) on 11 July 1874. Unfortunately I have been unable to find any record of William's life as a mariner in either the indexes of merchant seamen or the Lloyds Captain Registers. Very few ordinary seaman's records of service were kept from about 1857 to 1918, and unless the ships on which they served are known it is difficult to trace their seafaring service, as in William's case. We do know however that he had become the harbour master in the port of New Quay by 1911.

Mary Anne gave birth to the first of their two sons in New Quay on the 26 April 1875, whom they named David Peter. Unfortunately he was to have a very short life for he died at just two years and two days old. His mother and father must have been devastated. Their first child, a son, dying at two years old, was a tragedy for the young couple.

Their second son, John Lewis, was born in 1879, also in New Quay. This young John grew up and chose a profession totally unconnected with the sea, becoming a stonecutter. He did not confine himself to working in and around the locality of New Quay, however as in 1901 he was living in Toxteth Park, Liverpool. Liverpool had a population of some 685,000 at that time and was expanding at a very fast pace, the city boundaries having to be continually extended outwards. A stonecutter was in an ideal position to take advantage of the new employment prospects there.

By the time the 1911 census was taken, John Lewis had moved

back to New Quay and was living with his parents at 20 Marine Terrace. William and Mary Anne continued living here until their deaths, William dying in 1930 and Mary Anne six years later, in 1936. They were both buried at Llanllwchaiarn church graveyard in New Quay and are recorded on Mary Anne's family gravestone.

Jane, their second child, was born in 1856 also in St Dogmaels. We already know from the 1871 census that at the age of fifteen she was looking after six of her siblings at 18 Park Street, New Quay, while her mother was probably visiting her father in Cardiff. The ages of those siblings ranged from two to twelve years. She was obviously considered a responsible young girl.

Jane, as per the family tradition, was also to meet and marry a mariner. He was thirty-two-year-old Benjamin Williams whose home was in Alltfach, St Dogmaels. His father's name was also Benjamin. They married in Cardigan Register Office on 14 February 1884. Benjamin by this age already had many nautical miles under his belt having been at sea from the age of fourteen. It would be fair to surmise that he began his seafaring career sailing out of Cardigan as young boys did in those days. In early 1869 he was a crewmember of the Beaumaris ship *Jessie May* and in late October that year signed up as an ordinary seaman on the Swansea brigantine *America*. His voyage on this vessel began in Swansea on the 31 October and took him to Pernambico and Para in Brazil before returning to Liverpool in early May of 1870. The outgoing cargo she carried was probably coal, as Welsh coal in those days was in huge demand by the worlds ever increasing fleet of steam ships and steam engines. On St David's day 1872 he was again signing up, this time as an able seaman, on another Swansea ship, the 235-ton brig *H.H.* (The owner of this vessel was Henry Hoskins, hence the ship's name). This voyage also took him across the Atlantic, but the first port of call was the busy port of Cadiz in Spain, where a cargo of welsh coal could easily be sold. Cadiz's most famous exports then were salt, sherry and wines produced in the Andalucía region of Spain.

The *H.H.* could well have filled up her holds with any of these cargoes for the crossing of the Atlantic to Carboneaur in Newfoundland, and probably found them easy to dispose of.

Newfoundland's most famous export of course was timber, a much-needed commodity in South Wales, therefore this could have been her cargo for the third leg of her round trip back to Swansea, where she arrived on the 31 July 1872. In which case the owner of this vessel, Mr Henry Hoskins, would have made a healthy profit and Benjamin Williams added two Atlantic crossings to the many he already had and would make during the course of his seafaring career.

Benjamin was by now a very experienced sailor and in January 1882 he secured the post of boatswain on the Liverpool steamer *Hispania*, a ship owned by J Ellis and Co. A boatswain is basically a ship's officer who is in charge of the sail and rigging etc., a position ideally suited to Benjamin with his previous experience of sailing ships. The *Hispania* was a 263-ton vessel and was employed in the foreign trade. Benjamin served on her for the next eighteen months and a total of five voyages, ending his service in the port of Liverpool in November 1883, about three months before his wedding day. He most probably would have rushed home to St Dogmaels after being paid off.[3] There were many exciting things waiting for him there, not least his future wife who would have been delighted to see him. Christmas was coming and his Mam was at home at Alltfach ready to spoil him.

A Life at Sea

After the wedding Jane settled down to family life in St Dogmaels, and Benjamin before long returned to sea. A mariner's life and work usually takes them away from home for long periods of time and Benjamin's was no exception. He would still make regular visits home to his young family however. Their first child David was born in 1884, followed by Margaret Jane in 1893 and Benjamin John two

---

3 How would he have travelled to St Dogmaels from Liverpool? Did he sail on one of the little ships that ran a regular service from there to the Cardiganshire ports or did he travel by train? The railway system had built up a head of steam in those days and was rapidly expanding to some of the most remote parts of the United Kingdom. It would have been possible at that time to travel all the way from Liverpool to Crymych by train. The railway had reached Crymych in the mid 1870s almost ten years before it arrived in Cardigan. In the meantime a daily service of a horse-drawn wagon was used for passengers and goods making the onward journey all the way to Cardigan.

years later.

In 1891 Benjamin applied to be examined to become a mate on Home Trade Passenger Ships. He sat the examination in Liverpool in mid-June and was duly successful; his Certificate of Competency qualified him to be a mate on any vessel in the coasting trade, including those carrying passengers. As always, an application form had to be completed for examinations of this kind in which the applicant declares some personal details and as much provable seafaring experience as possible. Benjamin states that he was born in St Dogmaels on 4 November 1850 and his address when he made the application was Union Street, Liverpool. He also declared nine years of previous service at sea from 1882 to 1891. The vessels on which he had served during this period and the positions he held on them are as follows:

Name of Ship	Port of Reg.	Position held	From/to	Trade	Owner
SS *Hispania*	Liverpool	Boatswain	Jan 1882/ Nov 1883	Foreign	J.Ellis
SS *Rhinderen*	Cardiff	Able Seaman	Mar 1884/ Jun1884	Foreign	J.Cory & Sons4
SS *Stag*	Hartlepool	Able Seaman	Jun 1884/ Dec 1884	Foreign	Jackson Bros & Cory
SS *Swan*	Liverpool	Boatswain	May 1885/ May 91	Foreign & coastal	J.Ellis

By January of 1891 Benjamin was first mate of the SS *Swan*. This vessel was mainly employed trading between Liverpool and London and visa versa, making one voyage every fourteen days. Of the twenty or so crew members that set off from Liverpool in mid-January of that year five were St Dogmaels men. They were the master, John Edwards, the first mate our Benjamin Williams, the boatswain William Thomas and able seamen Daniel Thomas and William Davies. This particular voyage ended in Liverpool on 31 January with all crew discharged and paid off. Benjamin as first

4 John Cory & Sons Ltd was a company that had its roots in Padstow, Cornwall and in the 1860s moved to the rapidly expanding port of Cardiff and the profitable business of exporting Welsh coal. (www.angelfire.com)

mate was on this occasion responsible for paying and signing off all crew members, writing his initials against each individual's name including his own. The average pay that the crew earned, on this voyage was £1. 8s. 0d. each. Benjamin, as first mate, was paid £2. 12s. 6d. I dare say that the *Swan* was prepared and cargo loaded as soon as possible to make her next round trip to London and that many of the crew that signed off on her last voyage would sign on again for her next. Benjamin certainly did. Surprisingly, in the section of the ship's document 'Agreement of Voyage and Crew' which describes all the daily provisions to be allowed to crew members such as meat, vegetables, bread, tea and coffee etc., the following words were written: 'Crew to find their own provisions'. This statement seems to indicate that all crew members had to provide their own food for the entire voyage of two weeks. The ship owners really were maximizing their profits in those days.

Four years later in November 1895 Benjamin applied to become 'Master of Home Trade Passenger Ship' and was again successful. The certificate of competency was issued on the 2 December. On this particular application form he gives a brief physical description of himself: five feet five inches tall, dark hair, dark complexion with blue eyes. The vessels that he served on between 1891 and 1895 were as follows:

Name of Ship	Port of Reg.	Position held	From/to	Trade	Owner
SS *Swan*	Liverpool	2nd & 1st Mate	July 1891/ Nov 93	Coastal	J. Ellis
SS *Africa*	Southampton	1st Mate	Nov 1893/Dec 1893	Coastal	Union Steam Ship Co.
SS *Faithful*	Liverpool	1st Mate	Dec 1893/Nov 1895	Coastal	J. Ellis

There was a three-month gap in Benjamin's service on the *Swan* and on the application form he explains that this time was spent ashore recovering from a hand injury. The SS *Faithful* was also employed on a regular coastal service between Liverpool and London. It seems that J Ellis had become a favourite employer of Benjamin's, as the SS *Faithful* was the third of that company's vessels he had served on thus far.

By 1896 Benjamin had moved his family to Liverpool from St Dogmaels.[5] Moving to this great City, one of the busiest ports in the United Kingdom, was no small step for his wife Jane. She had only lived in St Dogmaels, New Quay and for a short while in Barry Island. These were small friendly communities where she had the support of family and friends. Certainly the move to Liverpool would have been a daunting prospect for her. She had three young children to look after, would miss her friends and family and there were many more worries besides I'm sure, but this move had one big advantage that outweighed all her anxieties, which was that she and the children would see and spend much more time with their father. Things seemed to have turned out well for the family as they stayed in Liverpool for some considerable time and quite soon there were two additions to the family, Mary Hannah in 1896 and Thomas in 1898.

Jane and her family lived at 20 Cotswold Street, a Victorian Terrace in the Kensington area of Liverpool. The family was recorded living on this street in both the 1901 and 1911 censuses. On both occasions eldest son David was not at home as he too had become a sailor and was probably at sea. Their children Margaret Jane, Benjamin John, Mary Hannah and Thomas were all at home, the youngest three still in school in 1911.

On that census day in the spring of 1911 Benjamin was the master of the ship *Norfolk Coast*[6] and he, his ship and her crew were lying

5 Between 1851 and 1911 Liverpool attracted at least 20,000 people from Wales in each decade peaking in the 1880s and Welsh culture flourished there. One of the first Welsh language journals 'Yr Amserau', was founded in Liverpool by William Rees (Gwilym Hiraethog) and there were, reputedly, over fifty Welsh Chapels in the city.
6 The 'Norfolk Coast' was owned by F H Powell & Co. of Liverpool and Benjamin had worked on this company's ships for many years. This company had become a leader in coastal shipping in spite of the downturn in that trade and in 1913 amalgamated with two other Liverpool companies to form the Powell, Bacon and Hough Lines Ltd. They operated coastal, short sea passenger and ferry services around the coast of the British Isles. With Benjamin's qualification of 'Master of Home Trade Passenger Ships' this company was a most suitable employer and visa versa, he was a most suitable employee for them. This Company usually named their vessels ending in Coast as

up in the port of Rochester, Kent. He was sixty years old and had been a sailor since he was a young boy of fourteen. He had a long and distinguished career at sea behind him. Was he, perhaps on that day thinking of how much longer he would carry on? It seems likely, for he and Jane returned to their beloved St Dogmaels about 1914 to a life of retirement. They made their home in 'Brodawel' a house that was to remain in this family's possession for a considerable amount of time. Jane was denied the pleasure of living back in St Dogmaels for very long as she sadly died on 25 January 1918. She was interred at Blaenweun Chapel graveyard. Her husband Capt. Benjamin Williams lived until 24 November 1934 and according to the report of his death in the 'Cardigan and Tivy-Side Advertiser' he was in his eighty-fifth year. Although he had lived in retirement for the last twenty years, he had seen over fifty years service at sea. He was buried with his wife Jane in Blaenweun.

The following are Jane and Benjamin's five children in birth order:

David was born in 1884 and followed in his father's footsteps, choosing seafaring as his profession. Like his father he became an experienced master mariner, first going to sea in 1900. By that time David had been living in Liverpool with his family for four years and must have adapted to city life. If he had discussed his future working life with his father I dare say the conversation would not have been very long. With his family background, his father a master mariner, coupled with living in such an exciting vibrant port city as Liverpool it would have been a surprise if he had chosen anything else.

He went to sea at fifteen years of age and devoted his working life to seafaring. He sailed on a great many ships during his lifetime and worked hard to make his way up through the ranks, eventually in 'Norfolk Coast'. Other examples of their ships names were 'Carmarthen Coast', 'Western Coast', and 'Devon Coast'.

Powell, Bacon & Hough Lines Ltd. in 1917 was purchased by the Royal Mail Steam Packet Co. at a cost of £800,000. (£33,277,882 in today's money) and re-named Coast Lines Ltd. By 1951 they had acquired controlling interest in a large number of coastal shipping companies and possessed a fleet of 109 vessels in total becoming one of the world's largest coastal fleets. In 1971 Coast Lines were acquired by the P&O Group. (www.nmm.ac.uk/coastlines)

becoming a master mariner. In July 1906 he sat the examination to become a second mate. Surprisingly though, at a time when commercial sailing ships were in the last throes of their existence, the Certificate of Competency that he was granted enabled him to serve as a second mate on square-rigged sailing ships. He had sailed on one such ship previously, for two and a half years between 1902 and 1905, so I suspect with that experience behind him he felt confident of being successful in the examination, which he was. As usual he had to fill in an application form to sit the examination and his personal description as he described it on this form was that his height was five feet three inches, he had a dark complexion, with brown hair, blue eyes and no personal marks or peculiarities. Apart from the fact that he was two inches shorter this description was the same, word for word, as that written on his father's applications all those years before.

David was building some useful experience in his career since becoming a second mate and true to form for young seamen of this family he showed his keenness and ambition for life as a mariner by applying in May 1908, barely two years later, to become a first mate. He was again successful. This time he was examined to be a 'First Mate of a Foreign-going Steamship'.

In February 1911 David again showed his ambition when he made an application to sit the examination to become a master mariner, the ultimate goal of so many of these young Welsh men. Since becoming a first mate in 1908 David had not actually been employed in that capacity on any of the three ships on which he had sailed. He had been second and third mate but never first, so in the column on the application form where he has to declare this information he does write in clear handwriting that on each occasion where he had been employed as second or third mate, there had only been the ship's master more senior to himself. This meant that although his title was that of a second or third mate his duties had really been that of a first. David was clearly anxious that the examiners were made aware of this important fact. Most personal information on this application was similar to his previous applications, stating that he still lived with his parents at 20 Cotswold Street, Liverpool but had grown one inch in height and acquired a tattoo of a snake on his left arm. It seemed that most old sailors could boast a tattoo or two on their forearms, which somehow always gave them an air of intrigue. In which foreign and exotic destination, I wonder, did he acquire this particular tattoo?

David was successful, passed the examination and went on to forge a long and successful career as a master mariner. He later married and raised a family in Fraserburgh, Scotland. David was probably at sea in 1934 when his father died, since his wife represented him at the funeral in St Dogmaels. There was also a floral tribute from the grandchildren in Fraserburgh, Tom, Cari, Pat, David, Janet, Betty and George.

The following is a list of ships that David served on between 1900 and the date of his master mariners examination on 6 February 1911.

Ship's name	Port of Reg.	Ton	Position	Owner	Trade
SS *Hopeful*	Liverpool	786	O.S.	Alfred H Reed *	Home
SS *South Coast*	Liverpool	221	O.S.	Alfred H Reed *	Home
Craigisla (sail)	Liverpool	989	A.S.	William Nicol *	Foreign
SS *Welshman*	Liverpool	3670	A.S.	British & North Atlantic Steam Ship Co. Ltd.	Foreign
SS *Basil*	Liverpool	2092	A.S.	Booth Steamship Co. Ltd	Foreign
SS *Annie Hough*	Liverpool	551	A.S.	Samuel Hough Ltd	Foreign
SS *Lustleigh*	Plymouth	2092	A.S.	Unknown	Foreign
SS *Hilita*	Glasgow	648	2nd M	John Geoff *	Balkans
SS *Agberi*	Liverpool	2176	4th M	Sir Alfred Jones *	West Coast of Africa
SS *Roquelle*	Liverpool	1336	2nd M	British & African Stm. Nav. Co. Ltd [7]	– ” –

SS *Madeira*	Glasgow	1147	3rd M	– ” –	– ” –
SS *Teneriffe*	Liverpool	1148	3rd M	– ” –	– ” –
SS *Warri*	Liverpool	1558	3rd M	– ” –	– ” –
SS *Prah*	Liverpool	1592	2nd M	– ” –	– ” –
SS *Ventura de Larrinaga*	Liverpool	2970	3nd M	Larrinaga Stm. Nav. Co. Ltd.	Foreign
SS *Anselma de Larrinaga*	Liverpool	2633	2nd M	Larrinaga Stm. Nav. Co. Ltd.	Foreign

(OS = Ordinary Seaman   AS = Able Seaman   M - Mate)

Margaret Jane was born in St Dogmaels about 1893 and married George Thomas Jones, a farmer of that village. They had one son, George Herbert Jones, who went to London and became a banker after the Second World War.

Young Benjamin John

Benjamin John was born in 1895 also in St Dogmaels and just like his brother David was keen to go to sea. He became a ship's engineer. The 1911 census records Benjamin John as a sixteen-year-old schoolboy living with his parents in Liverpool. It's not certain when he actually went to sea and few details of his career exist save that in September 1921 he became a second-class engineer in the Merchant Marine Service, sitting his examination in Cardiff. The

7 The British & African Steam Navigation Co. Ltd., who at the time that David served, operated routes transporting passengers, cargo as well as mail to Tenerife, West and South Africa. There were also routes between South Africa, America and Canada. The Larrinaga Steam Navigation Co. Ltd. originated in Bilbao Spain and in 1863 operated passenger and cargo services from Liverpool to the Spanish colonies of Philippines and Cuba. After the Spanish/American war in 1898 they began registering their vessels in Liverpool and ran services to Montevideo and the River Plate. Much of their business in the 20th century was tramping in the grain trade. Both the above ships, 'SS Vetura de Larrinaga' and 'Anselma de Larrinaga' were requisitioned for troop carrying during World War One. By the 1960s it was the last (tramping) company of its kind in Liverpool.

Tramp Steamers operate without a schedule, going wherever required to pick up and deliver its cargo.

following are a few personal details that are given on this certificate of application: e.g. that he had moved back to St Dogmaels with his parents and was living with them in 'Brodawel', his father was his next of kin, he was five feet three and a half inches tall with blue eyes and brown hair.[8]

Two years later, in July 1923 Benjamin John became a first class engineer, also taking this examination in Cardiff. On 13 March 1924 he married twenty-eight-year-old teacher Selina Griffiths from St. Dogmaels. The marriage took place on the little island of Curacao situated a few miles off the coast of Venezuela; the British Consulate there conducted the ceremony. Selina's father was contractor Thomas Griffiths. The marriage in itself was not surprising as they were both of the right age and had strong connections with St Dogmaels, yet it was the place where they were married that get's one's attention. Why Curacao? What was happening there at that time? Was Benjamin John working in Curacao, and was Selina working there? Or did Selina travel out just for the wedding?

As always with events that happened so long ago answers are never easy to find. However, the history of the area gives some clues. Venezuela was becoming one of the largest exporters of oil in the world and one of the companies taking advantage of this was The Royal Dutch Shell Company. The little island of Curacao was a Dutch colony where oil refineries and storage tanks were being built. This meant that there would have been many oil tankers and other vessels of all kinds plying their trade in this area with many opportunities for well-qualified marine engineers.

Whatever the origins, Benjamin John and Selina's life together for at least the next fourteen or fifteen years was centred on their work in Curacao, interrupted only by visits home to St Dogmaels. Before long there was an addition to the family when their son David was born in mid-December 1924. Probably anxious to show little David to family and friends in St Dogmaels they made plans for the first of their visits back to Wales and did so in June 1926. The only

8 There seems to be a pattern forming here. Benjamin and his two eldest sons were very much alike in stature and looks, as were many mariners of this family. They were on the short side, had blue eyes and brown hair (one of Britain's few Welsh Prime Ministers, Lloyd George, when ribbed about his shortness of height and stature is reputed to have replied 'in Wales we measure men from the neck upwards').

realistic mode of transport for anyone crossing the Atlantic in the 1920's was a passenger liner and Benjamin, Selina and David sailed with the Royal Netherlands West Indian Mail Ship SS Venezuela on her voyage to Amsterdam calling in Plymouth, Devon where they disembarked. It is interesting to note that on the in-coming passenger list their 'Country of Permanent Address' was Curacao in the Dutch East Indies. It's not known how long they stayed with family in St Dogmaels on this occasion but however long it was I'm sure they would have been very warmly welcomed.

They returned to Curacao at a time when Venezuelan oil production was increasing daily[9], which surely meant a busy working life for Benjamin. Other visits were made back to the UK and St Dogmaels, all recorded on ships' manifests and lists of passengers arriving or departing. The following are some of the details: Selina and five year old David returned home in 1929, Benjamin returned to London in 1932 to sit his first class motor engineer's examination, and he again returned to St Dogmaels in 1935. Benjamin on this occasion was traveling as a first class passenger, a sign perhaps of the success he was achieving in Curacao and Venezuela. The following year, 1936, Benjamin and Selina were recorded at the port of Dover boarding the German ship SS Claus Horn bound for Curacao. And finally, in 1937 Selina again returned to St Dogmaels.

Mary Hannah married Edwin Davies, a butter merchant from Pontypridd. He was also a deacon at Blaenwaun Baptist chapel, St Dogmaels. Their only son Benjamin Haydn Davies became a teacher; incidentally he was this author's woodwork and metalwork teacher in St. Mary's Secondary Modern School Cardigan in the 1950s.

Thomas, the youngest of Jane and Benjamin's children was born in 1898 in Liverpool and went into banking, working for Barclays

9 It had been known that Venezuela had an abundant supply of oil in and around 'Lake Maracaibo' since pre-Columbian times. The indigenous peoples had always made use of oil that had seeped to the surface for medical and other practical purposes. However it was not until 1912 that the first oil well was drilled and 'Royal Dutch Shell' and 'Rockefeller Standard Oil' were the first major producers. By 1929 Venezuela became the world's largest oil exporter.

Bank in Ebbw Vale during the 1930s.

Margaret, the third of Jane and David's children, was born on 20 December 1858 in New Quay and as previously stated she moved with her family to Barry Island, returning to New Quay by 1871. It may have been no surprise to her family that Margaret also went on to meet a mariner whom she wanted to marry, after all both her elder sisters had done so. She did marry on 20 December 1888 in Towyn Chapel, New Quay and her husband was twenty-seven-year-old Benjamin Williams from St Dogmaels. Benjamin's father, who incidentally was a mason, was also named Benjamin. It seemed quite ironic that Margaret and sister Jane both married men with the same name, both of whom were mariners, both from St Dogmaels and both of whose father's names were also Benjamin. This was a coincidence indeed.

A young Margaret Williams (nee Evans)

Without doubt Margaret's Benjamin was a mariner as this is recorded on their marriage certificate. There were few records of ordinary seamen kept during his time spent at sea unless the ships they served on were known. In Benjamin's case we are lucky that some records that refer to his life at sea do exist. Firstly, the census returns for 1891 and 1901 record that he was not present at their family home in St Dogmaels on both dates. This absence perhaps suggests that he was at sea on each of these occasions. There are also two surviving documents that refer to his service in 'The Royal Naval Reserve Force'. The first is his Certificate of Discharge from that force. It records that the date he first joined was 17 December 1880 and that he was discharged on 18 December 1910. He was awarded a gratuity of £50, a well-deserved reward for 30 years of loyal service. His rating at discharge was 'Trained Man, Fireman Class'.[10]

The second of the two documents unfortunately is not titled. It records details of his service in the naval reserve between 1896 and 1900, such as physical description, attendance at drill, retainer payments and ships served in the merchant service during that period. His physical description as recorded is that he was 5 feet 5 inches tall with a fresh complexion and hazel eyes. Like so many of the old sailors he was fond of his tattoos. He had a bracelet tattooed on his right wrist, an anchor and his initials B W on the back of his left hand, and the Union Jack on his left arm. The most interesting of the information on this document of course are the ships that he served on during this time. Between May 1896 and May 1897 he served on the little Cardigan registered steamer *Seaflower*, which ran a regular cargo service between Cardigan and Bristol at the time. (The *Seaflower* is referred to later in this book) In 1898 he served on a small Cardiff registered steamer *Lincolnshire*, a ship of about 60 tons operating cargo services out of ports such as Cardiff, Newport and Bristol. The third vessel recorded in this document is the *Speedwell* on which he served in 1900. There were many ships operating by this name at that time, and without knowing its registration number it's impossible to determine which of these ships Benjamin served on.

The following are Margaret & Benjamin's nine children in birth order

Margaret and Benjamin settled and raised their family in the village of St Dogmaels, at first in Church Street and later in the High Street. In the period from 1889 to 1900 Margaret gave birth to nine children and the details of their births are meticulously recorded in their family Bible. For instance, not only were the date and place of birth recorded but also the exact time of the day. Mary Jane, the first

---

10 A 'Royal Naval Reserve Drill Battery' complete with a 64 pounder gun existed at Glantivy St Dogmaels from 1867 to about 1906. Glantivy is situated on the south side of the river Tivy between St Dogmaels and the beach at Poppit. In August 1914 The Royal Naval Reserve were called to serve their country in the Great War.

born, saw the first light of day on 2 October 1889 at 2 a.m. in New Quay (the only child born outside St Dogmaels). Written over this entry were the sad words 'Wedi Marw' (Has Died), and in a later entry are given the details. Mary Jane had died on 14 December 1889 at just over two months old. She was buried at Blaenweun Chapel Churchyard, St Dogmaels. The following are the birth details of Margaret and Benjamin's nine children, all but Mary Jane being born in St Dogmaels:

Mary Jane	2 October 1889 at 2 a.m.
William	26 April 1891 at 2 a.m. (Willie)
David	11 November 1892 at 5 a.m.
John	26 September 1894 at 5 a.m. (Johnny)
Benjamin	25 September 1896 at 8.30 a.m.
Evan Roderick	17 September 1897 at 7.00 a.m. twin
Thomas Picton	17 September 1897 at 8.00 a.m. twin (Tom)
Jane Olwen	6 October 1898 at 4 p.m.
Lewis	5 October 1900 at 3 a.m.

In 1911 Margaret was still living at 1 High Street with her surviving children. Nine-year-old Jane Olwen had also sadly died in October 1907. She too was buried with her sister Mary Jane in Blaenweun. Of the surviving children, twenty-year-old William had moved out of the family home, David and John (Johnny) were carpenter's assistants, Benjamin was a shoemaker's assistant and the other three were at school. Incidentally, 1 High Street was a five-roomed property in 1911 and they had at the bottom of their garden a 'Twlc' (pigsty). Raising a pig or two in the back garden was a cheap and necessary way to provide meat to a large and growing family in those days.

Three years later, on 4 August 1914, Britain declared war on Germany and two of the boys, David and Benjamin, answered the call to arms. Thomas (Tom) joined up later in the war and Fourth son Johnny did what his father and his ancestors had been doing for decades and turned to the sea, joining the Merchant Navy Service. What must Margaret have been thinking, with three of her boys marching off to this 'war to end all wars' and another off to sea at the most precarious of times? She must have worried about them every minute of the day and night. She had reason to of course, since four of her sons were going off to the most dangerous places. Sadly, the war was not going to be kind to her family.

Margaret had already suffered the death of two of her daughters but more distress was to come. The first of the four tragic events that Margaret encountered during the course of World War I was not as a consequence of the war itself; it was something much closer to home. On 19 July 1916 her husband Benjamin died after a very short illness. The following is the report of his death in the Cardigan and Tivy-Side Advertiser on Friday 21 July:

"Taken ill at Haymaking - On Saturday last, Mr Benjamin Williams of 'Rose Lynn' St Dogmaels was assisting at the haymaking at Graig farm, when he was suddenly taken ill. He was removed home and Dr Stephens was called for, who ordered his removal to Swansea Hospital. This was done on Tuesday. When on arrival at that institution, his condition was found to be so serious that an operation was performed almost immediately. On Wednesday morning however, death supervened. The deceased was 54 years of age and leaves a widow and seven children, two of whom are in the army. The body was brought home yesterday (Thursday), and the funeral takes place on Monday at 2 p.m."

It is not certain of the cause of death, but it is generally thought in the family that he died from heart failure. He was interred at Blaenweun chapel cemetery with his two daughters.

Third child David enlisted into the Eighth Battalion, Royal Welsh Fusiliers in 1914 at Aberdare. This battalion soon moved to Blackdown, Hampshire for training, where they received orders to embark for the Mediterranean. They landed on Cape Helles, Gallipoli during July 1915. There they took part in the Battles of Sari Bair, Russell's Top, Hill Sixty and operations at Suvla Bay. They were evacuated from Helles between the eighth and ninth of January 1916 and were positioned along the Suez Canal defences by the end of that month. In February 1916 the division that included David's Eighth Battalion Royal Welsh Fusiliers moved to Mesopotamia[11], where they unsuccessfully attempted to relieve the besieged town of Kut. The town fell into the hands of the Turks who were then allies of Germany. During the course of 1916 the division was reorganized and later took part in the successful Battle of Kut al Amara.

The following is a brief summary of the report written by the Officer Commanding Eighth Battalion Royal Welsh Fusiliers, Lieutenant Colonel A. Hay, and records details of the Battalion's actions during the month of January 1917 *(Courtesy of the Royal Welsh Fusiliers Museum, Caernarvon)*:

Private David Williams – Royal Welsh Fusiliers – killed in action in Mesopotamia

"Between the 12th and 24th of the month the Brigade moved up to the front line and took over the left section of defence. Orders were received that the enemy's trenches opposite this line were to be captured and digging operations were commenced. The ground between the two lines was perfectly flat with very little cover and men digging were under continuous sniping fire. Notwithstanding great difficulties two continuous lines were finally established at a distance of 350 yards from the enemy. This represented a move forward of 650 yards and the digging of 5 miles of

11 Mesopotamia (now known as modern day Iraq) was formerly part of the Turkish Ottoman Empire and it is thought that Germany for many years before the war had developed Turkey as an ally. The Turkish army was often led by German advisers during World War 1. The British interest in this area was oil of which she relied heavily to keep her navy at sea and quickly occupied the oil fields near Basra in order to protect those interests.

trenches. *The attack was finally ordered to be delivered on the morning of the 25th. This attack was successful though a number of casualties occurred in crossing 'No Man's Land' including two Company Commanders."*

It was during this battle that David was killed. He was awarded the Victory Medal and British War Medal and is commemorated on the Basra memorial. (Note: During the current climate of instability in Iraq the Commonwealth War Graves Commission have made alternative arrangements for commemoration and produced a two volume Roll of Honour listing all casualties, which includes David's name, at their Headquarters in Kent. These volumes are on display at their Headquarters in Maidenhead and are available for the public to view).

Private Benjamin Williams killed in action aged 20

Fourth Son Benjamin volunteered to join the Fifteenth Battalion Welsh Regiment in Cardigan around August 1914. He was given a service number of 200492, a number allocated to the Territorial Army unit in St Dogmaels. This suggests he was a member of that unit before joining the Welsh Regiment. After training, the Fourth Battalion eventually sailed from Davenport for the Dardanelles, Turkey on 19 July 1915, landing at Souvle Bay on 9 August. It was soon after this that Benjamin contracted a fever and was repatriated home to recover. On 18 February 1917 he was drafted to France to join the 15th Battalion Welsh Regiment. He saw action at the Third Battle of Ypres and it was here during the battle of Pilckem that twenty-year-old Benjamin was killed in action, on 26 July 1917. He was awarded the Victory Medal and the 1915 Star. He is commemorated at the Bard Cottage Cemetery, Belgium. (Memorial Reference 111. F. 10.)[12]

At the end of February 1918, barely six months after the death of the second of her sons to die in the Great War, Margaret received another telegram, and this telegram, as was reported in the Cardigan & Tivy-Side Advertiser, 'plunged her and her family again into deep anxiety'. This devastating news came from the owners of the ship SS *Bay Kerran*, on which her son Johnny was serving. The SS *Bay Kerran* was a general cargo vessel and a very busy ship as would be expected during wartime. In the year or so before arriving in Cardiff on 24 May 1917 she had been trading in the Atlantic and the Mediterranean. On inspection of her 'crew list' for this period Johnny was not a crewmember before this date, so it is almost certain that he joined the *Bay Kerran* whilst she was loading her cargo, (probably of coal) at Cardiff. Unsurprisingly, Johnny was not the only man from the St Dogmaels area to do so. The tradition of men from West Wales of 'going to sea' was still very strong at that time and Cardiff was one of their favourite ports to sail from.

The two young men who signed up with Johnny were seamen Henry Pope and fifteen-year-old Emlyn Isaac, both from Cardigan. All three probably knew each other and may have travelled together by train to Cardiff. The SS *Bay Kerran* sailed from Cardiff in the middle of May and continued her usual trading pattern in the Mediterranean and the Atlantic, arriving in New York in early January 1918. There she loaded a cargo of grain and on the nineteenth of that month set sail towards her destination of St Nazair in France. Four days sailing out of New York the SS *Bay Kerran* found herself in heavy seas. The telegram Margaret received stated that the ship was about 500 miles from Nova Scotia when she got into difficulty owing to heavy seas and a wireless message was sent to that effect

12 The Battle of Passiondale began with an infantry attack by the allied forces on the 31 July 1917, but in the preceding two weeks much preparation was made, which included the bombardment of the German positions with four and a half million shells from 3000 guns. This still failed to destroy those heavily fortified German strongholds.

and to say that 'all her boats were gone'. This message was received by an American warship, which proceeded to the locality with all speed and patrolled for some considerable time, but found no wreckage. The ship was presumed to have sunk with all her forty-one crew perished, including of course poor Johnny and his two companions from Cardigan. On 3 April the SS *Bay Kerran* was posted missing at Lloyds and that is still the position today.

How grieved Margaret must have felt when that telegram arrived on her doorstep. The words 'plunged into deep anxiety' used by the Tivy-Side reporter must have come nowhere close to how she and her family felt that day. In the previous eighteen months she had lost her husband and now three sons. Life can be very, very cruel. At the end of the First World War she must have been at a low ebb indeed. She had lost her husband and out of the nine children she bore in the 1890s only four remained. She was probably never the same woman again.

Little is known of Margaret's son Thomas (Tom) Picton's life as a soldier in World War I. In March 1918 the Tivyside Advertiser published a report of a memorial service held in memory of his brother Johnny who had died when serving on SS *Bay Kerran*. At the end of this report it mentions that Margaret had another son who was at that time in a military hospital in this country. This was certainly Tom Picton. The 'Absent Voters List - Pembrokeshire Division' for the year 1918 records that Pte Tom Picton of Rose Lynn, St Dogmaels was not available to vote as he was serving with the Fourth Battalion Monmouthshire Regiment. The cause of his hospitalization is not known (many service records of WWI servicemen were destroyed during the bombing of London in the 2nd World War).

Lewis, the youngest of Margaret's family, was born in 1900. In 1916 he began an engineering apprenticeship with Cardigan's formative Engineering Company. Established in 1854 the 'Bridge End Foundry Company' was, apart from being iron and brass founders, agricultural engineers, millwrights, manufacturers and repairers of such things as Engines, Water Wheels, Thrashing Machines,

Turbine Wheels and a myriad of engineering equipment for the agricultural and other industries in the town of Cardigan and its district. This company was very well respected in the area and an engineering apprenticeship with them would have held any young man in good stead for the rest of his working life, as it did Lewis. He completed his apprenticeship in December 1921 with a glowing reference, describing him as intelligent, reliable, and attentive, signed by W. E. Matthews, sole proprietor of the company.

It's not known where Lewis' life took him immediately after his apprenticeship ended but by 1924, like so many young men of this family, he had succumbed to the call of the sea. He had become the 4th Engineer on the 3851-ton London registered SS *Bankdale*.

SS Bankdale

This ship was owned by the London firm of Japp, Hatch & Co, a well-respected company of ship owners who had fingers in many pies in the shipping world, including ship broking and coal exporting. I have little information of the cargoes the *Bankdale* might have carried but it is known that the ship did visit the port of Marseilles, France on several occasions. Lewis left the ship twice, the first time in March 1925 and the second in May 1926, both times while in Marseilles. On each occasion he was given a glowing reference by the ship's Chief Engineer, which was signed by the Master. They spoke of him as 'a willing and hardworking junior, sober at all times and attentive to his duties'. Who could ask for a better recommendation? In such an occupation Lewis I'm sure would have met numerous fellow sailors and engineers and made friends with many. One such friend was Harrison, Chief Engineer on the ship SS *Grelstone*. Lewis received a 'Ship to Ship Marconigram' from him whilst on one voyage asking of his well-being, Lewis replied as follows also by Marconigram, saying:

'Thanks. all is well. had rough passage. hope to meet near future. Lewis'.

I dare say that it would have been very difficult to keep in touch with fellow sailor friends than it is today with all our modern technologies

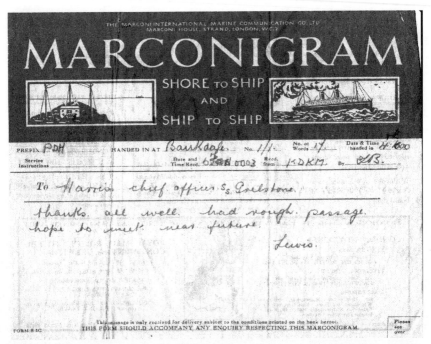

such as the internet, mobile telephones and computers etc. In the 1920s Marconigrams were at the leading edge of modern communications.

Lewis eventually returned to St Dogmaels to settle down and at some time during the 1930s teamed up with his brother Tom to start

LEWIS WILLIAMS ∴ Blue Glider Bus Service

AUGUST 1ST, 1951, AND UNTIL FURTHER NOTICE

St. DOGMAELS and CARDIGAN

From St. Dogmaels

a.m.	p.m.
8 45	1 45
9 40	2 30
10 40	3 30
11 40	4 30
	5 30
	6 30

No Service after 11 a.m. until 6 00 p.m. Wednesdays

From Cardigan

a.m.	p.m.
9 5	1 00
10 30	2 10
11 30	3 10
	4 10
	5 10
	6 10
	*9 15

* After Pictures. No Service after 1 00 p.m. until 9 15 p.m. Wednesdays

SATURDAY SERVICE

From St. Dogmaels		From Cardigan	
a.m.	p.m.	a.m.	p.m.
8 45	12 00	9 5	12 30
9 40	12 40	10 45	1 00
11 00	1 20	11 30	1 35
	2 00		2 30
	3 00		3 10
	4 00		4 10
	4 30		5 10
	5 30		6 10
	6 30		7 00
	7 15		9 15
	8 30		9 15

Saturdays. Bus leave Glanteifion at 1 50 p.m. and 5 25 p.m. | 1 35 p.m. and 5 10 p.m. run to Glanteifion

CIPPIN SERVICE

(SATURDAYS ONLY)

From		a.m.
St. Dogmaels	... ...	11 00
Gerazim	... ...	11 25
		p.m.
Cardigan	... ...	3 10

CILGERRAN to CARDIGAN

WEDNESDAYS

			p.m.					p.m.
Cilgerran	...	... dep.	5 45	Cardigan	...	... dep.		9 00
Penybryn	...	... „	5 55	Troedyrhiw	...	... „		9 5
Troedyrhiw	...	... „	6 5	Penybryn	...	... „		9 15
Cardigan	...	... arr.	6 10	Cilgerran	...	... arr.		9 20

SATURDAYS

			a.m.			p.m.				
Cilgerran	...	... dep.	10 30	1 00	2 00	3 20	5 00	6 15	7 30
Penybryn	...	... „	10 40	1 10	2 10	3 30	5 10	6 25	7 40
Troedyrhiw	...	... „	10 45	1 15	2 15	3 35	5 15	6 30	7 45
Cardigan	...	... arr.	10 50	1 20	2 20	3 40	5 20	6 35	7 50

					p.m.					
Cardigan	...	... dep.	12 15	1 30	3 00	4 15	5 30	7 00	8 30
Troedyrhiw	...	... „	12 20	1 35	3 5	4 20	5 35	7 5	8 35
Penybryn	...	... „	12 25	1 40	3 10	4 25	5 40	7 10	8 40
Cilgerran	...	... arr.	12 35	1 50	3 20	4 35	5 50	7 20	8 50

SUMMER TIME TABLE. Cardigan, St. Dogmaels and Poppit Sands

JULY, AUGUST and FIRST WEEK in SEPTEMBER

From				p.m.			
Cardigan	...	...	1 00	2 10	3 10	5 10	6 10
St. Dogmaels	...		1 15	2 20	3 20	5 20	6 20
Poppit	...	...	1 30	2 30	3 30	5 30	6 30

A timetable of the Blue Glider Bus Service in 1951

a new bus company, at first running bus services around the local districts of St Dogmaels and Cardigan.

I dare say that Lewis' engineering apprenticeship at the 'Bridge End Foundry' and his experience at sea as an engineer was a great advantage to the new bus company as vehicles of that time were so unreliable and temperamental. They needed constant tweaking and repairing, unlike of course the modern vehicles of today that hardly need a service from one year to the next.

Meanwhile, poor Margaret picked herself up and gained strength, if only for her remaining sons. She became the driving force behind Lewis and Tom's new company the 'Lewis Williams Blue Glider Bus Service', while Willie and Evan both went to work for British Rail in Aberdare and Swansea. Margaret died a well-respected member of the community on 14 February 1943. She was buried with her husband and family in Blaenweun Chapel cemetery, St Dogmaels. No less than seven ministers attended at her funeral and tributes were paid to her as a good mother and a faithful member of her chapel.

John Davies Evans was Jane and David's fourth child and first son, born in Barry Island in 1861 and possibly named after his paternal grandfather John Davies. His grandfather, following his young grandson's progress, must have thought him a real chip off the old block. Although he was born in Barry Island he spent most of his young life in New Quay, his father's home village, where the whole community was in one way or another involved with the sea. In practically every other household lived a sailor or a master mariner. The village would have been awash with stories of the sea, ships and far away places and would have excited any young lad that lived there. Every time he visited his paternal grandfather in the 'Sailors Home', St Dogmaels I suspect all the talk there would have been of the sea. His grandfather may have been a retired master mariner but he still owned the little sloop *Ellen Owens* and John's uncle William was her master. So what were the chances of little John pestering his uncle for a sail on *Ellen Owens*? Pretty high I'd say and his wish was probably granted. With this background it isn't surprising that young John Davies Evans became a sailor. After researching some of his maritime records it is clear to see that this boy was not only determined to go to sea but also to do well in his chosen career.

It was no surprise, therefore, that John went to sea at twelve years of age and on the *Ellen Owens*. Under the wing of her master, Uncle William, John began his seafaring career on 19 March 1873 and for the next eight months and three days was employed on this little Cardigan registered sloop as a 'boy'. The *Ellen Owens* was a small vessel of 34-tons and normally had three crew members: a master, mate, and a boy. She operated out of Cardigan mainly in the coastal trade, so the typical destinations John would have visited were Bristol, Swansea, Porthcawl, Saundersfoot, and Caernarvon. The work was not easy, the handling of the ship's masts and rigging strenuous enough but also loading and unloading the cargo was heavy work, a real test for a young twelve-year-old. These eight months working on the *Ellen Owens* must have been an excellent grounding for his future career, where he would have learnt a great deal about sailing and in particular sailing the Welsh coast with all its intricate complexities.

On 22 November 1873 John left his duties on the *Ellen Owens* and after a short break went back to sea. He spent the next seven years sailing Aberystwyth-registered vessels before moving on to Liverpool, the port of choice for many of these young sailors. Aberystwyth as a port had developed in a similar vein to Cardigan. It had been one of the busiest in West Wales, as was Cardigan, but with the arrival of the railway, in this case during the 1860s, the slow decline of trade through its port began. Even so, there was still many ships registered at the port, and many of these sailed far beyond the coast of Wales.

John applied to be examined as a second mate in Liverpool in 1882 and was, as usual, asked to state all his previous experience at sea. It is interesting to note that he, on the appropriate document, emphasizes the fact that not only did he have sailing experience but that on every occasion that it was possible to do so he had gone back to school to better himself. The schools he attended could possibly have been some of the Nautical Training Schools that were in existence in port towns and cities at that time. The following is a shorter version of the original record of his sailing experience.

Name of Ship	Port of Reg.	Service and Rank
Ellen Owens	Cardigan	Boy (8 months 3 days)
		On shore at school
Maelota	Aberystwyth	Boy (8 months 20 days)
Integrity	Aberystwyth	Boy/OS/AS (16 months 26 days)
		On shore at school
Hetty Mary	Aberystwyth	Boy/OS (9 months 6 days)
Hetty Ellen	Aberystwyth	OS (10 months 19 days)
		On shore at school
Tenobian	Aberystwyth	OS/AS (16 months 23 days)
Rhuddlan Castle	Liverpool	AS (8 months 6 days)
		On shore at school
Dovenby	Liverpool	AS (14 months 12 days)

(OS = Ordinary Seaman AS = Able Seaman M - Mate)

When John sat the above-mentioned examination to become a second mate of square-rigged sailing ships in November 1882, he was twenty-one. His home address given on the application form was 20 Marine Terrace, New Quay. He had actually been at sea for seven years and twenty-five days and back to school for a total of one year nine months. He passed all subjects on which he was tested, the most important of these being navigation and seamanship skills. He was also tested for colour blindness. With his sailing experience and training it was not surprising that he passed.

In 1884 John's ambition and keenness once again clearly came to the fore when he became a first mate. In September 1886 he achieved the prize he probably had always wanted, ever since the first day he'd joined his uncle William on the *Ellen Owens*, when he attained his master mariner's certificate. The examination was taken in Liverpool and the actual certificate was forwarded to John via the 'Mercantile Marine' office in Aberaeron. How proud he must have been when he collected it.

John's next move, to Liverpool, was probably inevitable. He wanted to make something of himself and that was one place where there were many opportunities for all keen mariners. He had worked for many of the big ship owning companies in Liverpool such as WC Jarvis & Co, Peter Irdale & Co, and R. Hughes & Co, all owning large fleets of sailing ships. One of these ships was the *Carnarvonshire*, owned by R. Hughes & Co, a large vessel trading all over the world. Another was the 779-ton *Ullock* owned by Peter Irdale & Co. John didn't confine himself to working entirely for Liverpool owners though, and one example of this was William Wilson of Glasgow, owner of the barque *Ryevale*. In fact both John and his brother David sailed on this vessel, but not at the same time.

He became a master within a short space of time but the first opportunity to command his own vessel didn't come from Liverpool but from a little nearer home. In 1887 he became the master of the 396-ton Swansea registered *Emily A Davies*, an iron built barque owned by James Davies, Cwm Avon, Port Talbot. John was the master of this vessel for approximately two years. His first voyage was to South America, destination Guayoquil in Equador. Equador at this time was expanding her production of cocoa in a big way and as a result its exports of this product increased ten-fold, so returning with this valuable cargo perhaps could have been the expectations of the owners and shareholders on this particular voyage. The master of every ship is responsible for all matters concerning the vessel under his command, from preparing the ship for sea, the safety of her cargo and crew, navigating through the wind, storms and tides and much more besides. This was a very heavy responsibility and every master must be 'up to that task'. This twenty-six-year-old John Davies Evans from New Quay, with already fourteen years of seafaring experience behind him, must have been 'up to the task' to have been given this opportunity.

One of the most daunting of these responsibilities I imagine was the control and management of the ship's crew, and the *Emily A Davies'* Crew Agreement for 1887 bears this out. John was careful in choosing the two most important members of his crew; his first mate was William Rowlinson, a Welshman and his bosun Albert Noordenlos, a Dutchman. He had sailed with these two men on his previous voyage on the *Ryevale* and I dare say he knew their capabilities and felt he could trust them both. The cook was James Bessin, a thirty-six-year-old from Jersey. The remaining crew members were all able seamen made up of two Welshmen and two Irishmen. There were eight crew members on board when she set sail from Liverpool on 7 January 1887 arriving at their destination on 29 April some four months later. There were no major incidents, at least none reported in this document. It must have been a long and arduous journey with much hard work intertwined with long hours of boredom. Towards the end the crew must have wondered if it was all worth it, because the pay was not up to much either. The first mate earned £5 10s 0d, the boatswain and cook £3 10s and all the able seamen £2 10s each. This was not per day or per week but per month. They must have been ready to let off steam when they reached Guayoquil. The master had stipulated that there was to be no alcohol on board at the very beginning of the voyage, a normal rule for ships of the day.

A Restless Crew

The first problem came a month later while they were still in port when able seaman Thomas Jennings for some reason deserted his ship, closely followed a few days later by the trusted boatswain Albert Noordenlos and able seaman Thomas Jones. As if to add insult to injury able seaman Thomas A Ryan claimed that he was unable to proceed to sea through sickness. There seemed to be some doubt as to the validity of this claim because Alfred Cartwright, the Acting British Consul in the port, carried out an investigation. This investigation confirmed the claim to be correct and so Thomas A Ryan was paid off. This left the Emily A Davies four men short of an already small crew. The master soon set about signing up some replacements and I dare say he couldn't be too fussy about who he chose. Three men were found, Sen Koba (Japanese), Gottfried Brigg (Polish), and A Janssen (Swedish). It seems these three men did not have very good English, because the terms and conditions of employment they were signing up to had to be read to them. The Acting British Consul witnessed this and was satisfied that all three men had understood. On the day that these new crewmembers were due to report for duty only two of them did so, since Gottfried Brigg never did join the ship.

Soon the *Emily A Davies* set sail once again and headed north to the port of Manta, also in Ecuador. Curiously enough while at this port the above-mentioned Thomas A Ryan had somehow caught up with the *Emily A Davies* and re-signed as a crew member, probably to the delight of the master as he was short of crew for the return journey to Britain. The master's delight was short-lived however because seventeen days later and before setting sail for home Thomas A Ryan did not report for the homeward bound voyage. He had deserted the ship once again.

They set sail in late July sailing south down the west coast of South America, around Cape Horn then north towards home, but this leg of their voyage was not without its crew problems either. Soon after they set sail James Bessin the cook became very ill and died of a 'Diseased Kidney' on 15 September. It would be safe to say that James Bessin was buried at sea as was the case for most ship deaths in those days, the funeral service being conducted by the master, in this case John Davies Evans. Their first port of call on home ground was Falmouth, arriving there in late November. The *Emily A Davies* was tied up here for fourteen days or so and nineteen-year-old Llewllyn M Lamb was employed for this duration, perhaps to assist in tidying and repairing the ship after a long rough passage. They again set sail, arriving in their final destination of the port of London, probably with a cargo of expensive cocoa beans, on 19 December 1887. Her crew, now amounted to four men of whom only two were original crew members. All were discharged here. John remained on the ship and must have breathed a sigh of relief and sat down with a cup of tea, or maybe cocoa, to gather his thoughts. The voyage must have been a baptism of fire for him in terms of managing the crew. I'm sure that he would have learned a great deal from it.

The fact that there was a death on board during the voyage had to be reported to the port authorities and the police. John carried out this duty on the first day of arrival and the following comments were written on the back pages of the Crew Agreement.

"It appears from the entry in the Official Log Book that James Bessin, Cook and Steward died of a Diseased Kidney on the 15th of September 1887. He appears to have been carefully attended during his illness. Signed: Joseph Watson, Superintendent 19.11.87"

In 1892 John married, and I don't suppose it would have been a surprise to anyone given his life, family and background that he married a master mariner's daughter. Her name was Elizabeth Lorenza Morris Jones, daughter of Captain Evan Morris Jones of Moylon, Rhydlewis and his wife Mary of Blaensylltyn in the Parish of Brongwyn. I suspect that they would have been happy that their daughter was to marry a young man with such fine prospects. The wedding took place in Pontypridd, Glamorganshire on 1 December that year. John and Elizabeth's families would have known each other since Captain Evan Morris Jones had moved his family from Rhydlewis to New Quay some years earlier. Elizabeth was nine years younger than her husband, born in 1870 not on dry land as you might expect, but at sea somewhere off the coast of Peru. The 'Register of Births Marriages and Deaths of Passengers at Sea' for the year 1870 states that Elizabeth Lorenza was born on the ship *Joan Cunllo* on 11 February that year, and that her parents were Mary and Evan Jones. Evan was the master of the *Joan Cunllo* from about 1863 to 1871 and clearly his wife had joined him on this particular foreign voyage. There could have been many reasons I suppose, why Elizabeth was born at sea, perhaps this voyage had been delayed and was taking longer than anticipated, or perhaps little Elizabeth simply arrived early.

Much care is taken today, quite rightly of course, of a pregnant mother and her baby, pre- and post-natal. Obviously this was not the case for Mary, in fact far from it. She had been at sea for several months of her pregnancy, if not all of it, on a relatively small sailing ship of only 298 tons, where you would be hard pushed to find any sort of comfort or privacy at all. Seasickness would enhance the morning sickness many times over. No anti-natal clinics to attend, no other woman on board, let alone a midwife to assist at the birth or to administer pain relief. There must have been many moments on this voyage when she longed for the comfort and security of home and to have her family around her. Mary would need courage to pull through such discomfort and hardship. She must have been a very strong woman, both mentally and physically.

Around 1892-93 John Davies Evans became the master of the *Ullock*, the Liverpool-registered vessel owned by Peter Irdale & Co, and one of the voyages he undertook on this ship began in 1893 and continued into 1894. The destination was already familiar to John for he had been there at least on one previous occasion, to Guayoquil, Ecuador. Little detail of the voyage is known except for the following; that on the 30 January 1894 whilst the *Ullock* was sailing off the Island of Puna in the Gulf of Guayoquil, Captain John Davies Evans died suddenly from Yellow Fever. This tropical disease is transmitted by the bite of some mosquitoes and was particularly rife in the nineteenth century. John and his crew really were in the danger area to contract this awful disease. The dangers of sailing, of wind and weather were not the only hazards sailors faced in those days. It must have come as a devastating blow to Elizabeth, his bride of barely fourteen months and to his mother who had experienced the death of her other son David four years earlier. John Davies Evans is remembered on his family's gravestone in Llanllwchauarn Parish Church cemetery, New Quay.

Elizabeth Lorenza's father, Evan Morris Jones, although related to this family by marriage only, is worth considering briefly if only to demonstrate how seafaring families in those times in West Wales became involved with each other, not only with their common interest of the sea but in particular through marriage. Evan was a vastly experienced sailor born in 1829 in Rhydlewis and was at sea by 1845, starting his career as an apprentice on the Gloucester ships *Reynard* and *Exportion*. He was a seaman on the Cardigan ship *Priscilla Eliza* in 1851 and, as many had done before and after him, his sailing eye looked towards Liverpool. He become a mate there in 1852 and a captain in 1854. In his life he sailed to all corners of the world, including destinations such as Beirut, Gibraltar, Quebec, Boston, Calcutta, Hong Kong, and China. He also commanded many vessels, amongst them the *Jos Morondo*, *The Duke*, *Nobob*, *Joan Cunllo* and finally his last command *British Commodore*. He died in the Naval Hospital in Valparaiso, Chile on 29 September 1882 of throat cancer.

Ellen was Jane and David's fifth child and little is known about her except that she was born in 1863 in New Quay.

William was born on 25 January 1865, the sixth child of Jane and David; he was also destined to spend his working life at sea. Like his brother John Davies Evans he spent his boyhood days in New Quay where a large proportion of the male population were sailors. He himself went to sea at the tender age of twelve. The first few years of his career were very much in the same vein as his brother, beginning as a boy on a Cardigan coaster. His first day of duty on this coaster, the brigantine *Angelina*, was the 16 September 1876. For the next ten years he sailed on thirteen ships registered in twelve different ports such as Swansea, Cardiff, Aberystwyth, West Hartlepool and London. In April 1877 he joined the first of two Swansea-registered ships, the 98-ton schooner *Excel*, employed as her cook/steward. Young boys of this age were often given this job. How much cooking went on I don't know for ship owners of the day were a pretty miserly lot when it came to feeding their crews. The diet on the *Excel* probably consisted of hard biscuit, bully beef, salted meats and very little else. The *Excel* traded in home and foreign ports and this particular voyage began in Newport, Monmouthshire visiting Gibraltar, Mazagan in Morocco, Inverness, Middlesbrough and back to Wales and the port of Briton Ferry. Quite an experience I would imagine for such a young boy.

In April 1881 William became a crew member of the second of the Swansea vessels on which he served; she was the 532-ton barque *Evangeline*, a ship trading in foreign waters. This vessel had a special significance to William because he had known her very experienced master practically all of his life, his Uncle Evan Davies. The family connection did not end there as also on board was one of his cousins, Benjamin Davies from Moylgrove, Pembrokeshire, the son of another of his mother's brothers and the ship's boatswain.

Whether it was by coincidence or by design that William became a seaman on the *Evangeline* we will never know. William had many relatives at sea; it was highly likely that one day he would become a crew member on the same ship as one of them. Whichever way it was the *Evangeline* left Cardiff docks, quite probably with a cargo of coal, on the 1 May 1881 bound for San Francisco. She arrived there on 3 November. The Californian gold rush may have come and gone but San Francisco remained a very hectic and dangerous place in the 1880s, with its hotchpotch of nationalities, gambling dens and bawdy houses. The waterfront was no place for a young boy from New Quay to be walking alone at night but I'm sure that Uncle Evan kept a close eye on both his nephews. It would have been possible at that time for William to witness the arrival of a Wells Fargo stagecoach in the city as they were still in use, although they were soon to be superseded by the railroad and disappear altogether. All of these experiences were part of the growing up process for sailors such as William.

The *Evangeline* remained in San Francisco for almost two months. They set sail on the 28 December and headed south down the Pacific coast of South America, around Cape Horn and set their course to the north once again, towards their next port of call St Nazaire on the French Atlantic coast. This had been a long and arduous voyage of five months and everyone must have been pleased when they set eyes on the French coast, arriving at St Nazaire on 25 May 1882. This was the end of Williams' voyaging on the *Evangeline*. He said good-bye to Uncle Evan and his cousin Benjamin and signed off.

Steam Supersedes Sail

As steam-powered trains superseded the stagecoach in America, steam ships were slowly superseding the sailing ships at sea. William went with the flow and in February 1883 became a steward on the Cardiff steamer SS *Forest*. He continued sailing both steam and sailing ships for a few more years and sat the examination to become a second mate in December of 1886 in London. On this application form he meticulously recorded his previous experience at sea for each individual vessel, such as the name of the ship served on, type, tonnage, official number, port of registry, position held, date of commencement and termination and whether it was in coastal or foreign trade. He also included a personal description of himself; he was five feet four inches tall with dark hair and hazel eyes. He was successful in the examination and became second mate on vessels that were registered in ports such as Antwerp, Boston, St Johns Newfoundland, Liverpool, and London. One of these vessels was the SS *Parkgate*, a 1435-ton steamer owned by the London based Turnbull Scott & Company. This Company always named its ships with the ending 'gate' as in 'Parkgate' and 'Nethergate' etc. Their fleets of ships were mostly tramp steamers with the exception of a small number that were employed transporting grain from the River Plate ports. William signed off from the SS *Parkgate* in London during September 1890 and a month later became a first mate, taking his examination again in London. In 1892 he became a master mariner, perhaps an achievement he had set his sights on since he was a boy. What a proud moment it must have been for the Evans family. Both elder sons had now become master mariners.

William married Alice Kate Patrick in 1897 in Fylde, Lancashire. Alice's family had been living in New Quay since the beginning of the 1800s and, given the close-knit community there, the two families would have known each other well. Alice in the 1911 census was living in Tan-y-Bryn, New Quay and had given birth to three children: John Patrick born in 1899 and Jane Doris in 1902. Helen Constance Patricia came along in 1914.

John Patrick was known locally as Jack Pat, a colourful character still remembered in the village to this day. He was the landlord of the 'Black Lion' public house and the poet Dylan Thomas, while holidaying in New Quay during the late 1940s, was a regular customer there. New Quay was popular in those days with the Welsh art and literary set and much is written about the raucous and drunken times at the Black Lion.

Curiously enough, although he was formally qualified to do so, there is no surviving record of William actually being engaged as master of his own vessel. In early 1918, when the end of the First World War was but a few months away, he was employed as first mate on the 1,330-ton ship SS *Kenmare*. On 2 March of that year while sailing twenty-five miles north west of the islets of Skerries, Anglesey she was torpedoed without warning by a submarine and quickly sunk with the loss of twenty nine lives, including that of the master Peter Blacklock. William was very lucky to be among the survivors, however during the incident his master mariner's certificate was lost. He wasted no time in applying for a replacement and this was delivered to him at an address in Cork on 3 May. On this application he lists nine ships that he had previously sailed on. The first three vessels were sailing ships on which he sailed before 1901; he was employed as mate on all three. The others were all steam ships registered in Liverpool. The position he held on each of these was of a junior officer.

One could easily forgive any sailor who had experienced what William had gone through on the SS *Kenmare* putting off returning to life at sea, but William was obviously made of stern stuff. I don't know exactly how soon he did return, but what is known is that he was the second mate on the 1,412-ton ship SS *Inniscarra* sailing out of Cork on 12 May, a mere two months after his experience on the SS *Kenmare*. The SS *Inniscarra* on this day was sailing ten miles south east of the Ballycottin Islands when again she too, without warning, was torpedoed by a submarine and sunk with twenty-eight lives lost. Unfortunately for William and his young family at home in Tan-y-Bryn this time he was not amongst the survivors. To survive the sinking of one ship could be considered very lucky, but to survive the sinking of a second in exactly the same manner would have needed a miracle, one that didn't arrive for William on that day. This was a poignant ending to forty-one years at sea, man and boy.

The following are William and Alice's children in birth order

Of William and Alice's three children, John Patrick (Jack Pat) married a lady named Elizabeth. Jane Doris never married. Helen Constance Patricia married a John F Lloyd and had two children, David Charles Patrick and Patricia Ann. Young David Charles Patrick was born in 1944 and followed in his grandfather's footsteps, making seafaring his career. As far as is known he was the very last person in this entire family to have done so. Details of his life and career are patchy to say the least. He was a twenty-one-year-old crew member of a passenger liner on a voyage from Australia to the UK in 1965. He was later a ship's mate on the *Tasmania Star*, a refrigerated cargo liner and one of the fleet of ships owned by the Blue Star Line. Around 1970 David settled to a new life in New Zealand, where his career flourished. He qualified as a master mariner and was employed as a marine pilot. He married Gillian Margaret; they had two children, Sacha and Gareth. David died a young man of thirty-three years of age in 1977.

Hannah, the seventh of Jane and David's children, was born in New Quay in 1867. Unfortunately, like her sister Ellen, little is known about her life. She died on March 29 1897 at thirty years of age.

David was the eighth of Jane and David's children, born in New Quay about 1869. There are no prizes for guessing the occupation he was to choose as, just like his two older brothers, he went to sea. There is no detailed information of David's life at sea, therefore it's not known exactly at what age he left home to begin his seafaring life. As previously mentioned, there were few records kept of ordinary seamen at that time. The one detail that was recorded regarding David was unfortunately not about his life but sadly about his death. David's working life at sea and indeed his whole life was a short one and details of his death were recorded on the Board of Trade's list of Deceased Seamen in 1888. He was eighteen years old when he died on the 11 October of that year.

The cause of death was given as inflammation of the brain. Other details recorded were that he was an ordinary seaman serving on the sailing ship *Ryevale* and this vessel at the time of his death was actually at sea about fifty miles west of the Cape Verde Islands. His home address was 20 Marine Terrace, New Quay, Cardiganshire. This was, as we know, his mother's home, the place to where he would always return. David was the first of her two sons to die at sea during her lifetime. There must have been much sadness within his family when the news finally arrived in New Quay.

Evan was Jane and David's ninth child, born in 1873 in New Quay and, like all young boys of this family, he answered the call of the sea. He joined the barque *Victoria* as an apprentice in February 1888 at fifteen years of age. This vessel was owned by Richards Bros. of Prince Edward Island, Canada. They owned a large fleet of vessels, many of them barques employed in the supply of copper and metal ores to the many smelting works that existed in the lower Swansea Valley at that time. Swansea was indeed nicknamed Copperopolis, a reflection of the fact that at the height of its production it smelted two thirds of all the copper ore imported into Britain. It is not known at which port Evan first joined the 748-ton *Victoria*, the first of three vessels belonging to this Company he was to sail. The other two were the *Mabel* and the *Genesta*.

He completed his three-year apprenticeship on the *Victoria* in February 1891 and within two days signed on to serve on the *Mabel*. Both vessels were very similar and both were registered in Charlotte Town, Prince Edward Island. During the following four years Evan sailed on a further four ships, including the 1451-ton SS *Glanhafren* owned by the Cambrian Steam Navigation Co. of Aberystwyth. This company's owner John Mathias entered into the world of steam shipping in the 1880s and mainly traded coal from the South Wales ports to the Mediterranean and Black Sea.

In 1895 Evan become a second mate and two years later a first mate. The examinations were taken in the Port of London and he was successful in both. Clearly Evan felt ambitious and confident at this stage of his life for within a short period of six years, in 1903, he had sat the examination to become a master mariner, again in London. Again he was successful, becoming the third of Jane's sons to have done so. Of course, a sailor that held the relevant ticket to be a master of a ship did not always automatically become master of the next ship that he sailed.

Many sailors, even to this day possess higher qualifications than their currently held positions. If there are no suitable vacancies available at the time one has to wait until the opportunity arises. This is perhaps what happened to Evan. In the spring of 1911, he was recorded on that year's census return as the mate of the ship SS *Rockabill* tied up in the port of Newport, Monmouthshire. The

Shell Oil tanker 'SS Trophon'

Rockabill was a 1,611-ton steam ship and Evan was the senior person on board that day, the master not being present and it seemed that the full compliment of her crew were absent too. There were only four men besides Evan: one sailor, a cook, and two stewards. A steam ship of this size would have required many more crew members. Nellie, the wife of the steward John Johnson was also on board, presumably taking a rare opportunity to spend some time with her sailor husband.

Nothing is known of Evan's seafaring life from 1911 until about 1920 when he served on the ship SS *Oliva*, a vessel owned by The Anglo Saxon Petroleum Co. Ltd., a subsidiary of the Royal Dutch Shell Oil Company. A year later he was the first mate of the 3,847-ton SS *Trophon* also owned by the same company, As the name suggests, both these vessels were oil tankers. On 17 June 1921 the SS *Trophon* set sail from the port of Glasgow on a voyage that took her to the near Continent, the Mediterranean, Caribbean and Mid and North America. Some of the many ports visited were Malta, New Orleans, Montreal, Trieste in Northern Italy, Colon in Panama, Tampico in Mexico, New York and Rotterdam. The ship's three most senior positions, the master and the first and second mates, were all New Quay men. The master was thirty-four-year-old Daniel Jenkin Stanley Evans, the first mate was our Evan Evans and the second mate was twenty-seven-year-old Evan Otway Jones, later to become a well-respected master mariner in his own right.

The SS *Trophon's* Official Log at the time Evan was a member of her crew contains many entries and reports made by the master during the course of the voyage. They range from the everyday routine occurrences to the most serious of incidents. The following are three examples from which one could glean an inkling into life on board:

"On 22/2/1922 R. Purvis was promoted from Able Seaman to Boatswain raising his wages to £13. 10s. 0d. per month."

Another, of a far more serious nature, happened on 8 March 1922 at 10.48 a.m. in the Gulf of Mexico. The report begins:

"This vessel slightly grounded and Engines immediately stopped and soundings taken around the vessel. Casts showing 3.5 fathoms forward, 4 fathoms amidships and 4.5 fathoms aft. Bottom soft sand. 10.54am full astern engines, and at 11.00am vessel refloated. Continuous soundings taken and engines worked cautiously to Master's orders, feeling way to deeper waters. 2.04pm vessel in 9 fathoms of water, engine full ahead. 2.30pm vessel in 12 fathoms of water proceeded on voyage. No apparent damage done. Signed The Master and First Mate."

There was of course the perennial problem of crew behaviour, or in this case the lack of it, for the ship's officers to deal with. Quite often the root of these problems was drunkenness while on shore leave. The following records an incident that occurred in the port of Colon, Panama:

"At 1.30am on 15.3.1922 it was reported to the Officer on Watch by H Friday, sailor, that D Hill, Fireman, was severely assaulted, whilst asleep in his bunk by T Skinner, Donkeyman(Stoker). On making enquiries it was found that T Skinner walked quietly into the Forecastle, armed with a Galley Poker and attacked D Hill beating him repeatedly about the head and body and was stopped with

difficulty by the members of the crew, the Poker being taken by Mr. Jones 2nd Officer. It being a most murderous assault the doctor and police were immediately sent for and D Hill was taken to hospital for medical attendance. T Skinner being taken to Prison by the police. Further, a Revolver was found by the police which was alleged to be T Skinner's property. The vessel was ready to sail at 5.30am but was delayed through having to attend the trial of these men, each being fined 10 Dollars as they had previously been fighting on shore. On the advice of the British Consulate, as the other members of the crew had declared they would not sail with T Skinner, I left these two men behind in prison. According to medical advice D Hill was unfit to proceed on voyage. The balance of their wages was deposited at the British Consulate, the amount being T Skinner £22. 7s 0d and D Hill £10. 8s 3d. Their effects were taken to prison by the two men. Both men were under the influence of Liquor at the time of assault and when taken from the vessel. Signed, The Master and First Mate."

These latter two incidents of course were not daily occurrences and were to be avoided if at all possible, but they do highlight the qualities needed of a master and his team of officers to deal with all situations that arise on board ship, whether at sea or in port. Evan was promoted from first mate to the master of the SS *Trophon* later in 1922 and remained so into 1923. Sadly, in January 1925 while at home with his sister Mary Anne at 20 Marine Terrace, New Quay, Evan contracted pleurisy and pneumonia and died, on the fifteenth of that month. It was recorded on his death certificate that he was a seaman in the Merchant Service. He bequeathed all of his effects to his sister Mary Anne.

Thomas was the tenth and final of Jane and David's children. He was born in 1876 also in New Quay. I have been unable to find many details about his life apart from the fact that the 1891 census returns record he was a fifteen-year-old apprentice tailor living with his mother at 20 Marine Terrace.

Anne and Mary, John and Mary Davies' second and third children (twins)

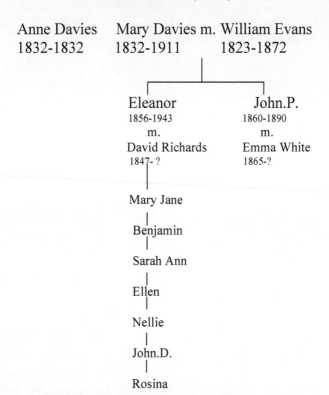

Anne Davies   Mary Davies m. William Evans
1832-1832   1832-1911   1823-1872

Eleanor   John.P.
1856-1943   1860-1890
m.   m.
David Richards   Emma White
1847- ?   1865-?

Mary Jane

Benjamin

Sarah Ann

Ellen

Nellie

John.D.

Rosina

CHAPTER 3

Mary and Ann (twins) - the second and third of John and Mary Davies' children

Mary and Ann were twins, born in Cardigan on 3 April 1832. They were the second and third of John and Mary's children. They too were baptized in Capel Mair but unfortunately Ann died in infancy, in contrast to her twin who lived to a grand old age. In 1841 Mary was living with her family, at Panteg. By 1850 she had met her future husband and yes, he was a mariner, William Evans, a twenty-eight-year-old originally from Aberayron, Cardiganshire. They married in St Dogmaels Parish Church in June of that year. Their first home was one of the cottages that were attached to her family home of Panteg, next door to her parents. In the spring of 1851 the census returns show she was the sole occupier of the cottage, her new husband probably having gone back to sea. At least she had plenty of family around for company whilst he was away on those long voyages.

Mary gave birth to a daughter Eleanor in early 1856, followed four years later by a son, John Phillip. By 1861 Mary and the children had moved to High Street, St Dogmaels. She was described as a master mariner's wife in the census return of that year. Phoebe James from Aberporth was employed as a servant in the house. William was again not present; the reason was almost certainly that he was away at sea.

William by now had become a busy and experienced mariner. Even though he had been born in Aberaeron, another village with a small port on the Cardiganshire coast, he seems to have begun his seafaring life at Cardigan in 1837 at the age of fourteen. Cardigan at that time was still a very busy port with a great number of ships registered there, so there were an abundance of vessels in the port on the lookout for prospective apprentices as well as many keen young boys looking for the opportunity. William was one of these boys. His three-year apprenticeship was served on the Cardigan registered 70-ton schooner *Prudence*, a vessel trading in home waters. Thereafter his career followed the general pattern of many of these young men from the Cardigan area that went to sea. At first he sailed on Cardigan vessels, then spent a period sailing from ports further afield before returning to Cardigan once again. The following is a list of ships he sailed on and the ports they were registered in, covering the years 1837 to 1855. This list is taken from his application to become a Master Mariner in 1855.

Ship	Port of Reg.	Position	Trade
Prudence	Cardigan	Apprentice	Coastal
Favourite	Cardigan	Seaman	Coastal
Aeron	Cardigan	Master	Coastal
Catherine and Jane	Cardigan	Mate	Coastal
Eliza	Lancaster	Mate	Coastal
Rover	Stockton	Seaman	Coastal
Walter	Liverpool	Second mate	Foreign
John and Henry	Cardigan	Seaman	Foreign
Elizabeth	Cardigan	Mate	Coastal
Ann Letitia	Cardigan	Mate	Coastal
Neptune	Cardigan	Master	Coastal

Voluntary examinations for sailors who wished to become master mariners or mates of ships were introduced in 1845 and became compulsory in 1850. The men who passed were given Certificates of Service. These were also issued to those masters and mates who were exempt from the examination by reason of their long service. William applied for his Certificate of Service citing his long service as master. The application was sent to the 'General Registers and Record Office of Seamen' at Customs House, London in August 1855. A letter from that office was sent by return of post to the Shipping Master at Cardigan stating that they could find no record of William in any capacity above that of a mate prior to the application being made. They informed that they would issue him a certificate for 'mate only', if proof was not found of his service as master. William provides the proof needed in the form of two letters from former employers. The first, from Merchant Samuel Jones, managing owner of the sloop *Elizabeth* of Cardigan, states that William had been the master of that sloop on no less than four occasions between September 1847 and January 1850. The second was from three other of the *Elizabeth*'s owners: Morgan Rees, William Williams and Thomas Griffiths, also testifying that he had been her master before 1851. This was proof enough for he was issued with his Certificate of Service in February of 1856.

It was about this time William became the master of the 60-ton schooner *Hero*. This vessel had been built in Chepstow in 1820 and in the thirty-six years or so of her existence she had been through the mill once or twice. For example, in 1837 she had been lengthened, extensively repaired and her mast rebuilt. In 1852 she had a new deck fitted and some large repairs carried out. In 1855 she underwent more damage repairs. She was described in the Lloyds Register of Shipping as a Cardigan Coaster and her registered owner was Evans & Co.

The following ten years could be considered Williams' Greenock or River Clyde period because all the vessels that he served were registered at that port. In the years 1860-61 he served on the brigantine *Rambler*, a ship whose destined voyages during that time were from the River Clyde to Newfoundland. Between 1862-64 he served on the schooner *Vine*, her destined voyages being from the Clyde to Seville in Spain. It wasn't until 1866 that William seized his best opportunity since he had arrived on the Clyde six years earlier. This was given to him by Warden & Co., an ambitious firm of ship owners that were trading from Greenock. They had in this year added a brand new vessel, the *Aberfeldy*, to their existing fleet. William was chosen as her master. She was a schooner of some 141 tons and ninety feet long, not a large vessel but William was well versed in sailing small schooners as previously indicated. This experience perhaps was the reason that Warden & Co entrusted this new vessel to him. The *Aberfeldy*'s voyages during her short lifetime were mainly between ports on the Clyde and South America. In 1870 while en-route from Huelva[1] in Southern Spain to Glasgow with a cargo of copper ore she got into difficulty off the coast of County Wexford, Ireland and was wrecked. The circumstances of the incident or the fate of her crew is not known except that William Evans did survive. This was the last of the Greenock ships he was to sail.

Not disheartened by this misfortune William soon went back to sea, becoming master of the ship *Coila* in 1871, a 175-ton barquentine owned by the Liverpool ship owners Doward, Dickinson & Co. On 19 April 1872 the *Coila*, with William now her master, undertook a voyage that took them into the Baltic Sea. Unbeknown to him this was to be his last and final voyage. They were to call at any port required, returning to the United Kingdom in a time not exceeding six months. When one examines the list of her five crew members the first thing that comes to mind is they were all hand-picked men. Amongst them were two men from Aberayron, two from St Dogmaels and one from Cardigan.

The practice of a ship's Captain choosing a crew from the towns or villages from which they came was quite common and none more so than those from West Wales. They could always find good experienced men there to crew their ships. Williams' mate was his namesake William Evans also from Aberayron, his boatswain was William Rees from St Dogmaels and his cook was seventeen-year-old David Selby from Cardigan. On 25 May they arrived in St Petersburg, Russia where they remained for over one month. It was during this time that William began to feel unwell. The following was written in the ship's Official Log by William Evans the mate:

---

1 The Province of Huelva was known for its copper ore deposits and one of the important mining companies operating there in 1873 was the British owned firm of Rio Tinto.

"Monday June 24th at 6 am. (St Petersburg)

6am Capt. William Evans took ill. Doctor was sent for by the request of the Master.

7am Doctor came on board and reported the Master very bad.

2pm the Doctor came on board and reported the Master in the Cholera.

4pm the Doctor was sent for and reported that the Master would not live long.

5pm the said Master died.

Signed;   William Evans…Mate

William Rees…Boatswain

Evan Evans…Able seaman

Tuesday June 25th at noon (St Petersburg)

The said William Evans was taken to the dead house

Wednesday June 26th (St Petersburg)

The body of the said William Evans was buried

Signed;   William Evans …Mate

William Rees…Boatswain

Evan Evans…Able seaman

Saturday June 29th (Cronstad – a small island situated off the coast of St Petersburg)

William Evans Mate of the Brigantine 'Coila' was appointed Master of the said vessel in the place of William Evans who died at St Petersburg. Signed by the British Consulate in Cronstad"

William Evans gathered together and listed his late master's belongings as follows;

3 shirts, 6 draws, 9 waistcoats, 3 pillow cases, 7 coats, 8 trousers, 10 pairs of stocking, 5 sing lets, 4 mufflers, 1 sheet, 1 blanket, 1 rug, 3 hats, 1 oilskin coat, 1 sou'wester, 2 bags, 3 pair of boots, 1 pillow, a compass, charts and tables.

The *Coila* set sail for home immediately after being signed off by the British Consul, now under the command of her new master. One additional crew member had been signed on to make up the shortfall; his name was Charles Stenburg, a Russian. What he made of all the Welsh spoken on the little vessel we will never know. They arrived at Plymouth on 5 August where all the relevant paperwork and reports were delivered to the Shipping Master and all crewmembers signed off except for one, her new master. When walking away from the *Coila* the crew must have thanked their lucky stars that they had not contracted cholera too. They had come perilously close.

Life at sea was not the late William's only occupation. In January 1868, probably while home on leave between his comings and goings from the Clyde to South America, he made what later proved to be a very wise decision, becoming the landlord of the 'White Hart' Public House in St Dogmaels. I believe that during his time at sea his wife Mary was more than capable of running this public house. She was living there when the terrible news came through of her husband's death. There isn't much one can say or do to console anyone for the loss of a husband or wife except to support and help and there would have been plenty of family in St Dogmaels to do just that.

The children, Eleanor and John Phillip were a big help to their mother I'm sure. On 1 November of that year William's personal estate and effects were awarded to his widow by administration. I wonder if William's belongings that had been so carefully listed by his mate William Evans in St Petersburg ever reached Mary in the 'White Hart'.

William's decision in 1868 was the beginning of eighty years of this Evans family's association with the 'White Hart'. Mary became the landlady after her husband's death and remained so until her death in May 1911 aged seventy-nine years. For the last few years her granddaughter Sarah Ann Richards had assisted her in the day to day running of the White Hart, but it was her daughter Eleanor Richards who became the next publican.

Eleanor had married David Richard, a carpenter from Llanllawby, Carmarthenshire, in 1874. The 1911 census shows she had given birth to eleven children although only six survived.[2] At the time of her mother's death she was living with her family in Cardiff. She then moved back to St Dogmaels to take over at the White Hart. She remained there as the landlady until her death in January 1943, at the grand old age of eighty-eight, beating her mother's age at death by nine years. The following is an extract from the report of her funeral in The Cardigan and Tivyside Advertiser:

> *"Another link with the past has been severed of a highly respected inhabitant in the person of Mrs Eleanor Richards, White Hart. The deceased was a faithful member of Capel Degwel Congregational Chapel". She was buried in the Parish Church St Dogmaels".*

The above Sarah Ann Richards, daughter of Eleanor, followed in her mother's footsteps and became the last of the women from this Evans family to become landladies of the White Hart. Her sister Rosina Richards married Percy William Osborn from Bristol in the spring of 1930 and moved away from St Dogmaels for some time, but by 1948 had returned to live with her sister in the White Hart. She sadly drowned in the river Tivy in the autumn of that year. Soon after the death of her sister, a distraught Sarah Ann put the White Hart up for sale. She herself died the following year aged sixty.

William and Mary's second child was **John Phillip**, born in St Dogmaels in 1860. He became an Elementary School Teacher. By the age of twenty-three he had moved to the little village of Giant's Grave near Briton Ferry in Glamorganshire, where he held the post of Certificated Teacher in the local 'Mixed and Infant school'. In an

---

2 Only seven of Eleanor's children's names are known to the author, therefore these seven only are recorded in the family tree.

entry in the school's Daily Register, on 27 April 1885, it was recorded that he had become a Certificated Teacher of First Division Second Class. In short, he was beginning to advance in his chosen career.

In December of the following year John married Emma White, daughter of a sea pilot from Giant's Grave. The marriage took place at Neath Register Office. For a few years after the wedding it seems John did not enjoy the best of health. The school's Daily Register reported that in October 1889 he went home from school early one afternoon suffering from a violent headache and face ache, remaining off school for several days. In early April 1890 John was off school again, this time suffering from a serious attack of bronchitis. He remained off school until early May when it was recorded in the register on the ninth of that month that he had died. The following day the school was closed and all the pupils were taken to his funeral.

What a sad end to this young man's life. He had worked hard and seemed to be making progress in his chosen career. He had been married for a mere four years and seemed to have a bright future ahead of him. It seems very sad that his life was cut short at such a young age and was especially tragic for his wife Emma.

John, John and Mary Davies' fourth child

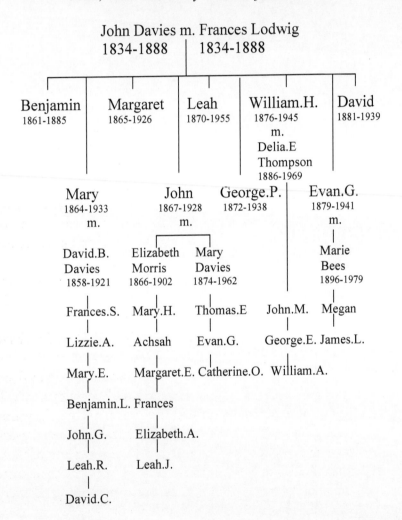

John Davies m. Frances Lodwig
1834-1888 | 1834-1888

Benjamin
1861-1885

Margaret
1865-1926

Leah
1870-1955

William.H.
1876-1945
m.
Delia.E
Thompson
1886-1969

David
1881-1939

Mary
1864-1933
m.

John
1867-1928
m.

George.P.
1872-1938

Evan.G.
1879-1941
m.

David.B.
Davies
1858-1921

Elizabeth
Morris
1866-1902

Mary
Davies
1874-1962

Marie
Bees
1896-1979

Frances.S.

Mary.H.

Thomas.E

John.M.

Megan

Lizzie.A.

Achsah

Evan.G.

George.E.

James.L.

Mary.E.

Margaret.E.

Catherine.O.

William.A.

Benjamin.L.

Frances

John.G.

Elizabeth.A.

Leah.R.

Leah.J.

David.C.

CHAPTER 4

John – the fourth child of John and Mary Davies

John Davies aged 17 (photo taken circa 1851)

John Davies was born on 24 October 1834 in the Bridgend area of Cardigan. He was John and Mary's first son Like his three sisters he was baptized in Capel Mair, Cardigan by its minister Rev. Daniel Davies of Moylgrove. Soon after his birth the family moved to Panteg in St Dogmaels and this is where John was brought up, practically within sight of the River Tivy.

As a child he would have witnessed the busy and thriving maritime business that occurred on and around this river at that time and would have known by name all the wharfs, quays, warehouses, lime kilns, granaries and shipyards at the busy port of Cardigan. He also would have recognized every locally owned vessel that sailed up and down the river; one of these was of course his father's 60-ton schooner *Thetis*. I dare say he knew her every nook and cranny from bow to stern; every sail and every rope would have been familiar to him. He would have learnt every knot and known his starboard from his port before his left and right.

Most young boys take a great interest in their father's trade whilst growing up and then perhaps discover interests of their own. John however retained his father's interests in ships and the sea into

THE FAMILY REGISTER OF _John & Frances Davies, Blaenywaun, Moylgrove, near Cardigan_

NAMES	WHEN BORN	WHERE BORN	WHERE & WHEN REGISTERED	WHERE & WHEN BAPTIZED	MARRIED	DIED
John Davies	Oct 20 1834	Cardigan	Cardigan Feb 6 1834	Capel Mair Jan 1st 1834	Sept 6 1859	Aug 4th 1888
Frances Lidberg	May 1836	St Dogmells	Cardigan June 20 1836	Capel Degol June 23 1836	July 6 1859	April 8th 1888
Mary Ann Davies	Dec 27 1861	Blaenywaun Moylgrove	Cardigan January 5 1862	Capel Degol March 20 1862	Married William Griffiths Nov 17 1885	
Mary Davies	Jany 12 1864	Blaenywaun Moylgrove	Cardigan January 2 1864	Henllywelan January 22 1864		April 25 1933
Margaret Davies	Oct 10 1865	Blaenywaun Moylgrove	Cardigan October 23 1865	Blaenywaun Oct 30 1865		Dec 1st 1926
John Davies	Oct 7 1867	Blaenywaun Moylgrove	Cardigan January 7 1868	Blaenywaun January 3 1868		Nov 23rd 1948
Lisa Davies	March 18 1870	Blaenywaun Moylgrove	Cardigan April 6 1870	Blaenywaun May 16 1870		March 21 1955
George Phillip Davies	Sept 27 1872	Blaenywaun Moylgrove	Cardigan Oct 14 1872	Blaenywaun Oct 15 1872		June 6th 1938
William Henry Davies	Jan 23 1874	Pontyvelam Moylgrove	Cardigan Oct 2 1876	Bethel Moylgrove July 30 1876		July 7 1943
Evan Griffith Davies	March 15 1877	Pontyvelam Moylgrove	Cardigan March 12 1877	Bethel Moylgrove		June 3 1941
David Davies	Aug 14 1880	Pontyvelam Moylgrove	Cardigan Aug 29 1880	at Pontyvelam		Feb 6 1939

adulthood and this became his life until his dying day.

In late March of 1851 when the National Census Record was taken sixteen-year-old John was living at home with his parents at Panteg. All the talk and gossip of the family I'm sure would have been of the sea, sailors and all the business that went with it. Like his father he had now become a sailor. There is no exact record at what age he first went to sea; it probably would have been around the twelve or thirteen year mark. Similarly, the name of the first ship upon which he sailed is not known but it may well have been his father's ship *Thetis*.

Photograph of the old cottage of Pantywylan

He continued his career at sea and by 1859 had met Frances Lodwig the daughter of master mariner Benjamin Lodwig and his wife Leah of Pantywylan, Moylgrove, Pembrokeshire. They were married on

6 September of that year. Pantywylan became John and Frances's home for the rest of their lives; a home that I believe brought much happiness to them and where they raised a family of nine children. Frances of course knew full well the consequences of marrying a sailor. The dangers and the long separations that were inevitable were familiar to her, having lived all of her life within her seafaring family.

The 1861 census showing the inhabitants of Pantywylan were:

Name	Relationship	Marriage	Age	Profession
Benjamin Lodwig	Head	Widow	59	Farmer and Master Mariner
Frances Davies	Daughter	Married	27	Master Mariner's wife
Margaret Lodwig	Daughter	Un-married	23	
Leah Rees	Daughter	Married	20	Master Mariner's wife
Benjamin Lodwig	Son	Un-married	18	Seaman
Titus James	Servant	Un-married	35	Servant on farm

Benjamin Lodwig at this time was master of the 117-ton schooner *Agenoria*, built in 1834 at Newport, Pembrokeshire. The registered owners of this vessel were Evans & Co. of Cardigan. Benjamin had been her master for the previous seven years and by 1862 he had acquired at least twelve of her 64 shares. The ship's Account of Voyages and Crew for the following year, 1863, records that his son-in-law John Davies had now became her new master.

John at this time was yet to sit the Board of Trade examination to become master but this was not at all unusual for this time. Benjamin himself had been a ship's master for many years before sitting his examination in 1851. Many ship's masters sailed all of their lives without a certificate in the old days.

The *Agenoria* was officially described in the Lloyds Registers as a Cardigan Coaster, since all her trading was being carried out

1 Official Number / Signal Letters	2 Ships' Names, &c.	3 Masters.	4 Regisd Tonnage (Net, Gross, Under Deck)	5 Registered Dimensions (Length, Breadth, Depth)	6 Engines of Steamers. Builders of Engines. Materials. Repairs of Ships, &c., if Cerused.	7 Build. (Where, Builders' Names)	8 Build. When	9 Owners.	10 Port belonging to.	11 Port of Survey.	12 Years, if Assigned.	13 Character if Assigned, for Hull and Stores. Also Date of Last Survey.
21	Africaine Iron	Scw J.Castan 5 B.lds	341 502	202·5|25·3|14·2 1'·44ons 1 D&Br.B.	1.2Cy.36"-27" 90 11P. MC.66 Bickwell&Gordn,P.Glsg	P.Glsg. Blackwd	1866 1mo.	Touache&C.	Mrselles	Cly. A.&cr.		12,66
2 68814 W.B.D.	African Iron	Scw Bg RW Dixon 6 B.Hds Cen.72	1258 2419 1887	315·7|34·3|16·3 P.93/1.F.53/1.24·1 2 Dks&r.B.	C.I3Cy.38"&70"-48", 60 1b.|2801 P. MC.73 J.Key, Kingœra	Knglm J.Key	1872 12mo.	Union Steam ShipCo.	Shmptn	Sou. A.&cr.		100A1 11,75
3	Afrique Iron	Scw Bg T.Ricce	834 1227	256·3|30·5|15·5	C.2Cy.33"&16"-36", 250 11P. Greenock Fndry Co.Guk	Grenck Scott	1872	Valery, frère & fils	Mrselles	Cly. A.&cr.		
4 68636 W.T.Q.	Afton Iron	Bk J.Semple 1 B.Hd Cen.75	848 866 822	204·9|32·3|20·1 R.Q.D38/1.F.28/1. 1 D&Br.B.	....	Glasgw Lan.&. Gls.Co.	1875 6mo.	D.Hunter	Ayr	Cly. A.&cr.		100A1 6,75
5 26291 P.K.M.R.	Agamemnon P.&dia.d.63 & YM.73	S R Marsden	1431 1431 1277	252·3|36·2|23·2 P.85/1.F.49·1/1. w.Nrsdsw	&d.63p.x&d.37srp.73 C.2Cy.30"&2"-52", 72 1b.] 300 11 P. Greenock Fndry Co.Guk	Londn Green	1855	R.&H.Green	London	Lon. A.&cr.	4	A 1 12,74
6 54924 M.K.G.B.	Iron	Scw Bk	1550 2279 2212	309·3|38·8|28·4	C.2Cy.30"&2"-53", ...	Grenck Scott	1865	Ocean Steam ShipCo.	Liverp'l	Liverp'l		
7 65673 V.R.P.C.	Iron	Scw Sp	19 127 127	106·3|18·8|10·0	L.2Cy.28"-45" 65 11P. Reathead,Soy&Loy&Co.	S.Shlds Reath'd S.Shlds	1872					
8 30376 K.N.B.	Agatha	Sr	112 112	85·5|19·4|11·2	....	Drtmth	1854	W.E.Denton	Clchster	Clchster		
9 22196 N.K.L.R.		Sw	187 187	92·9|23·6|13·5	....	Lynn	1859	J.Sutton	Lynn	Lynn		
30 54411 L.V.L.P.	P.& YM.74&.L	Bk P.Bastian	431 431 407	137·2|27·7|17·2 R.Q.D.35/1.	&rp.66&08	Sndrl'd Mills	1866 1mo.	Hankey&Co.	London srr.Ion.71	Lon. A.&cr.	13	A,75
1 50214 F.M.D.	Agenora YM.74pt G.I.B.	Bg E.Bartley	230	110·0|25·2|13·8	Cstiogp/8yrsMd. de Patron	Grnsey Patron	1865 10mo.	WPotter&Co ContGns Oct.74	Guernsy Gns. ContGns	A.&cr.	8 3	A 1 5,74
2 22381 L.G.B.	Agenoria pd I.R.	Sr J.Davies	84 90	66·3|20·5|11·2 &rp.52rp.61nn.	&rp.66pltnn.681·p.72	Nwprt	1834	J Davies&Co	Cardig'n Car.	Cardig'n Car.	10	4,72
3		S O.Griffith	996	178·8|36·7|23·0	....	N.Brisl	1855	R.Chapman	[Livern'l] Liv.	Liv.	7	

Lloyd's Register of Ships for the years 1876-1877 showing John Davies as Master of the Agenoria and J Davies & Co as the owner. *Courtesy of Lloyds Register Group Services Ltd.*

in 'Home Waters' (e.g. around the coast of Britain, Ireland and the near continent). Operating a wooden sailing ship such as the

Agenoria was not cheap. It would have been necessary to continually repair, replace, and service her tackle and equipment; such were the ravages of the sea on these little coasting vessels. It would become unavoidable, every few years, to make major repairs and alterations. The *Agenoria* was no exception, in 1852 she had been converted into a brigantine, and her size reduced to 84 tons. During 1861 some major repairs were carried out and in 1865 a new deck fitted. All this would obviously bite deep into the profits of the owners and shareholders, but it was necessary in order to keep a ship afloat.

The register 'Transactions Relating to Ships Register' for the port of Cardigan shows that in January 1865 Benjamin Lodwig sold by bill of sale twelve of the *Agenoria's* sixty-four shares to his son-in-law John Davies. From that point the registered owners of this vessel became J. Davies & Co. of Cardigan. (This was the same Company that also owned John's father's two vessels the *Thetis* and the *Ellen Owens*). In total, in 1865, there were fourteen shareholders of the *Agenoria* and the numbers of shares held by these individuals varied from two to sixteen shares.

Interestingly the person who held the greater number of shares was a man who had invested in numerous Cardigan ships and was well known to John. He was the Rev. Daniel Davies, minister of Capel Mair, Cardigan and the man who had baptized him all those years ago. The following are a list of ports the *Agenoria* visited in 1863:

Depart from	Date	Arrived at	Date
Limerick	14 February*	Crosshaven (Cork)	2 March
Crosshaven	10 April	Swansea	15 April
Swansea	30 April	Honfleur (Normandy)	6 May
Honfleur	18 May	Pau (South West France)	22 May
Pau	30 May	Runcorn	6 June
Runcorn	19 June	Bantry (County Cork)	6 July

*4 January – 14 February she was laying up at Limerick

Voyages in the second half of 1863 were not dated:

From:	To:
Garston (On the river Mersey)	Swansea
Swansea	Cork
Cork	Swansea
Swansea	Le Havre (Normandy)
Le Havre	Swansea
Swansea	Le Havre
Le Havre	Swansea

The *Agenoria* continued a similar pattern of trading to the above. The port of Swansea was the centre of her operations for the remainder of the time that John Davies was associated with her. In fact she was registered as a Swansea Coaster in 1869-70.

The total number of crew serving on the *Agenoria* at any one time was usually four, not including the master. The number of crew employed by the master during the above year totalled thirteen, of these two were Cardigan men, one from St Dogmaels, one from Aberporth, and two from Newport, Pembrokeshire. The remainder were from England, Ireland and Russia.

The main port in which crew members signed off and new crew were hired was Swansea, a very busy port during this time. Thousands of vessels would come and go taking cargoes of coal, tin plate, and copper to ports all over the world and there would have been a large pool of sailors for John to choose from. The *Agenoria* would also have carried similar cargoes to its destinations. The following order appeared in the Cardigan Workhouse 'Day Book' in June 1865 *(Courtesy of Ceredigion Archives, Aberystwyth)*:

Order: "That David Jenkins Shepherd be apprenticed to John Davies of Pantywylan, Moylgrove Master of the 'Agenoria' of Cardigan and that the sum of Twenty Two Pounds be paid to the said apprentice in the following manner, three pounds at the expiration of the first year, four pounds at the expiration of the second year, six pounds at the expiration of the third year and nine pounds at the expiration of the fourth and last year of the said tenure. That the Indenture of apprenticeship is prepared and the parties requested to attend at the next meeting of this Board."

This Indenture of Apprenticeship began on 29 June 1865 and it seems that things did not go entirely to plan. It was recorded in the ship's Account of Voyage and Crew Agreement covering the second half of 1867 that for reasons only known to himself David Jenkins Shepherd on 29 July deserted the ship while in the port of Swansea. For whatever reason David decided that life on board this ship was not for him and he set off to make his own way in the world. I wonder if he had been paid the £4 due to him at the expiration of the second year as deemed by the Indenture?

On 4 July 1870 John Davies sat his examination to become a master mariner in Dublin and was duly successful. The fee that John was charged for the certificate was two pounds. The National Census Return of 1871 was taken on 3 and 4 April recording the inhabitants of Pantywylan as follows:

Name	Relationship	Marriage	Age	Profession
Frances Davies	Head	Married	37	Farmer of 37 acres
Benjamin Davies	Son	Un-married	9	Scholar
Mary Davies	Daughter	Un-married	7	Scholar
Margaret Davies	Daughter	Un-married	5	Scholar
John Davies	Son	Un-married	3	
Leah Davies	Daughter	Un-marries	1	
Mary Phillips	Maid	Un-married	35	Maid

Of the Lodwig family that lived in Pantywylan ten years earlier only Frances now remained. Her father Benjamin and all her siblings had moved on to pastures new and Pantywylan had now become the home of this growing young Davies family. Frances and John had become parents of five children and, I dare say, were now a very busy couple. Frances was at home looking after the children while John was at sea making a living on the *Agenoria*. Three of the children were scholars and probably attended the Board School in Moylgrove with its brand new building, erected as recently as 1867.

In 1872 as far as the *Agenoria* was concerned everything seemed to be going along very well. The pattern of trading for this year was much the same as in the 1860s. John had again signed on a new apprentice, fifteen-year-old Thomas Williams from Moylgrove. On page five in the ship's Official Log, where the master is required to review the character of his crew and make comments, he reports that Thomas Williams' 'general conduct' is very good and that his 'ability in seamanship' is as yet only good.

The *Agenoria* in 1876 had a very late start to her trading year, as she was in need of some repairs. These were carried out in Cardigan, probably in one of the shipyards on the banks of the river Tivy at Netpool. On 5 June when all the work had been completed, John and his crew boarded her for the first time that year, setting sail for Cardiff the very next day. John would have been in a hurry to make some profit to pay for the repairs. It is interesting to note that this vessel's managing owner for this year was none other than his father John Davies of the 'Sailors Home', St Dogmaels.

Also serving his apprenticeship on board was his eldest son Benjamin. So, there were three generations of the Davies family involved with this particular voyage. Father, son and grandson, all members of J Davies & Co., working together.

1878 saw quite a big change in the life of the *Agenoria*, when John Davies appointed twenty-nine-year-old James Williams of Moylgrove as her new master. He took over the reins on 18 March while the *Agenoria* was laying up in Porthcawl, Glamorganshire. Other crewmembers who signed on that day were: Thomas James of St Dogmaels as mate, David James, John's son Benjamin Davies as able seamen and eighteen-year-old Henry Bowen as apprentice. Henry was the latest in a long line of apprentices that served their time on this vessel. On 7 November the mate Thomas James signed off at Cardiff and seventeen year old Benjamin Davies was promoted in his place.

To make up the shortfall in crew numbers, Thomas Edwards of St Dogmaels was signed up. Things went well for the *Agenoria* in 1878 and I suspect this could be put down to the efforts of the new master James Williams. Even so, the following year John Davies appointed yet another new master, promoting his son Benjamin to that position. This was very rapid progress up the promotion ladder for him, from mate in November of one year to master in March of the next. This appointment was short-lived however and only lasted nine months. On 31 December of that same year Benjamin moved on to pastures new.

Sail under Severe Pressure

With the increasing reliability of steam engines, shipping companies were finding that a steam ship was faster, more efficient and more reliable than its sailing counterpart and therefore more profitable. As a consequence more and more steam ships were coming into service, putting sailing vessels under severe pressure. The port of Cardigan was no different from any other small port in the 1860s, its livelihood under threat from competition in the form of the railway, due to arrive in the town in the near future.

In 1869 the 'The Cardigan Steam Navigation Co. Ltd.' was formed with the intention of entering the new era of steam. A new 64-ton vessel with the ability to reach speeds of ten knots was purchased and named SS *Tivyside*. The SS *Tivyside* was immediately put into a weekly service between Cardigan and Bristol carrying general goods. This service was a success and the company made good profits. In 1876 a rival company 'The Cardigan Commercial Steam Packet Co. Ltd.' was formed and like their competitors looked to the Clyde for a new vessel to operate out of Cardigan. They chose a slightly larger 73-ton vessel, the SS *Sea Flower*, which arrived in Cardigan during September 1877. The intention initially was to put her into regular service not only from Cardigan to Bristol but also to Liverpool. The Liverpool venture was short lived and irregular.

The reason John had appointed a new master of the *Agenoria* in March 1878 becomes clear on inspection of the SS *Sea Flower's* 'Crew List and Agreement'. It records that John had taken over as master of that little steamer on the very same day as James Williams had become the new master of the *Agenoria*. It seems John had been offered this prestigious position and after some consideration had decided to accept. His intention perhaps was to keep and operate the *Agenoria* alongside his work as master of the *Sea Flower*. His father at the 'Sailors Home' could have continued as her managing owner intending that his young son Benjamin would eventually become her permanent master.

For the next two years this was the case, but in 1880 things went drastically wrong. In circumstances not known the *Agenoria* was lost, but fortunately all her crew were saved.

John took over his new duties on the SS *Seaflower* on 18 March 1878 and the same day set sail for Swansea. How much experience he had of sailing steam ships at this point is not known. It was probably limited, and he must have been greatly helped by Thomas Jones, her previous master. Thomas continued his service on the *Sea Flower* for the next three months in the capacity of mate, probably to gently ease John Davies into his new job. During the year this little steamer made forty-five voyages to Bristol, one to Cardiff, one to Liverpool (all with general cargo) and one voyage to Swansea for coal. This was a very busy first full year of operations and certainly things did not always go smoothly.

While on a voyage between Cardiff and Cardigan in late November the *Sea Flower* was in collision with an Irish registered sailing vessel *Charlotte*. The *Charlotte*, with a cargo of potatoes, sank but thankfully her crew was saved by the *Sea Flower*. The *Sea Flower* however was deemed to be at fault and the owners had to pay compensation. As a consequence this put the Cardigan Commercial Steam Packet Co. into temporary financial difficulties. These were resolved in 1879 and both the Company and the *Sea Flower*, with John at her helm, operated successfully for many more years. She was a fast and reliable little steamer, her crew usually all from Cardigan and St Dogmaels, consisting of seven men, these being the master, mate, two able seamen, an engineer and two firemen.

The 1881 census return for Moylgrove shows three additional children had been born to John and Frances in Pantywylan since the previous census was taken ten years earlier. All were at home except eldest son Benjamin who was probably at sea. The inhabitants of

Pantywylan at the beginning of April 1881 were:

Name	Relationship	Marriage	Age	Profession
John Davies	Head	Married	46	Master Mariner
Frances Davies	Wife	Married	46	Wife
Mary Davies	Daughter	Un-married	17	
Margaret Davies	Daughter	Un-married	15	
John Davies	Son	Un-married	13	Scholar
Leah Davies	Daughter	Un-married	11	Scholar
George Davies	Son	Un-married	8	Scholar
William Henry Davies	Son	Un-married	4	Scholar
Evan Griffith Davies	Son	Un-married	2	

The Pantywylan Bible

Frances was pregnant for the ninth and final time when this census was taken in early April, as another son David was born 14 August that year. All the children's details were recorded on a page at the front of the Pantywylan family bible, showing when and where born, registered and baptized. It also notes the date that John and Frances were married, 16 September 1859. The last column on this page was set aside to record the family's death details. Unfortunately John and Frances did have to make one entry in this column, to record the death of their eldest son Benjamin who, in 1885 at the age of twenty-four, died at sea.

This death marked the beginning of a few years of sadness and unhappiness for the family. No sooner had they got over Benjamin's death they were struck with another tragedy, for in April 1888 their mother Frances also died. Then, just four months later, their father John died after a brief illness. The children must have been devastated and felt as if a rug had been pulled from under them. The two rocks in their lives that they could always depend on had been taken from them in just four short months. It was a very sad chain of events and must have sent them reeling.

John himself remained the master of the *Sea Flower* until his death and had become highly respected in the maritime and wider community in Cardigan, St Dogmaels, and Moylgrove. The following is his obituary in the Cardigan Tivy-Side Advertiser:

"DEATH OF CAPT. DAVIES, 'SS Sea Flower'. – The very sudden decease of Capt. John Davies, master of the 'SS Sea Flower', of this Port, which took place at his residence, Pantywylan, Moylgrove, on the 11th instant, after a brief illness, has cast a gloom over the whole district. During the period of 11 years, during which he had been master of the 'Sea Flower', he made himself, through his amiable disposition, and obliging and pleasant manner endeared to and esteemed by everyone that came in contact with him, and by his death the company have lost a good and faithful servant, and the crew a most kind master. The directors and officials of the Cardigan Commercial Steam Packet Company, to show their deep sympathy with the bereaved family in the irreparable loss they have sustained, and their high esteem for the deceased, attended the funeral, which took place on Tuesday, and was numerously attended. The Rev. W. Jones, Moylgrove, officiated at the deceased's residence, after which a procession was formed in the following order: – Directors of the 'SS Sea Flower', the coffin, mourners and a large concourse of the general public, the interment taking place at the parish churchyard of Moylgrove, where the Rev. E. Evans, vicar, officiated in the Church and at the grave. The coffin was borne from the Church to its last resting place by the crew of the 'SS Sea Flower', who were deeply affected at the sad ceremony imposed upon them. The deepest sympathy is felt for the sorrowing family."

John and Frances were buried together in St Peters Church cemetery Moylgrove and their memorial in the shape of a square column also remembers six of their children. Pantywylan remained in this Davies family's hands until the 1940s and was always remembered with warmth and affection by all the children no matter how far they roamed. Perhaps this was a testament to the loving and warm family home that John and Frances had created there.

John and Frances' children

John and Frances' eldest child **Benjamin** was born on 17 December 1861 at Pantywylan and was the only one of their nine children to follow the family tradition of going to sea. As previously noted he began his apprenticeship on board his father's ship the *Agenoria* in November 1874, at barely thirteen years of age. He served on her for over four years; the first three of these were as apprentice and thereafter he made rapid progress up the ranks, becoming her master in March 1879 when only eighteen. There were probably many reasons why John had faith and trust in his son to take charge of his precious vessel. He obviously knew him very well, had taught him all he himself knew, and seen first hand how he operated on board ship. Benjamin possessed a very good character, was a strong willed responsible young man, and above all was a natural sailor. As previously mentioned his reign as master was short lived, only for a period of nine months, but I'm sure a lot of experience was gained and lessons learnt which would have stood him in good stead for the future.

The experience Benjamin gained of the seafaring life in the four years or so he spent on board the *Agenoria,* must have made up his mind that this was the life for him. Despite that, in the next five months he was to take a break from the sea. Benjamin was not the kind to waste opportunities or time, as he indicates in his application to become a ship's mate three years later. On this particular application form he recorded that at least some of this time off was spent at school. The school that he mentions was I suspect a school for mariners that taught seafaring skills and navigation. As previously mentioned there were many of these schools in port towns and cities of the time and were usually privately run. In view of the fact that the next vessel that he was to join was a Swansea registered ship, the school he attended may have been 'White's Navigation School', one of the many existing in Swansea at that time.

Benjamin eventually went back to sea in May 1880, joining the Swansea-registered ship *Evangeline* as an able seaman. Like his cousin William Evans, who was also later to join this ship, he knew her master. He was Uncle Evan Davies, his father's brother. He knew Evan well, not only as an uncle but also as neighbour; Evan lived in the village of Moylgrove only a mile or so from Pantywylan. Did Uncle Evan encourage Benjamin to join his ship and suggest the navigation school? He was certain to have known of his sailing ability and that he had a bright future, so he may well have done. The *Evangeline* was a 532-ton Barque owned by Richards, Power & Co., a typical Swansea vessel employed mainly transporting copper ore and coal to and from that port.

Benjamin signed on the *Evangeline* in the port of Gloucester on 12 May 1880 and sailed on her for a period of nineteen months, signing off in Dublin on 14 November 1882. These were nineteen more months of very valuable experience gained under the guidance of Uncle Evan. During his service on this ship Benjamin was promoted from able seaman to boatswain, becoming a very proficient and knowledgeable sailor. Although this ship usually operated out of the port of Swansea, this seems not to be the case during Benjamin's time on board. The following is a list of voyages made by the *Evangeline* from May 1880 to November 1882. She in fact made eight Atlantic crossings and sailed twice around Cape Horn:

From:	To:
Gloucester	Baltimore (USA)
Baltimore	Calais (France)
Calais	New Orleans (USA)
New Orleans	Rouen (France)
Rouen	Cardiff
Cardiff	St Catharina (Brazil)
St Catharina	San Francisco (USA)
San Francisco	St Nazaire (France)
St Nazaire	Charleston (USA)
Charleston	Bermuda (North Atlantic)
Bermuda	Dublin

In January 1883 Benjamin sat the examination to become mate of a square-rigged sailing vessel and was successful. It is not certain on which ship he was employed until January 1885 when he became a crewmember of another Swansea registered vessel, the 384-ton *Pembroke Castle*, owned by the Simpson Bros. There were eleven crewmembers listed on the ships 'Agreement and Account of Crew' and Benjamin was listed as her first mate and second in command to her master, James Bevan. They set sail on 13 January, on a voyage that took them from Swansea into the Atlantic and south towards South America, their first port of call being Paysandú, Uruguay. The Crew Agreement describing the planned voyage ahead, stating they would "trade in any port or place within the limits of seventy-five degrees north and sixty degrees south latitude for the maximum time of two years, to end in the United Kingdom". This gave the master a wide range of options in which to trade that could have taken them from as far north as Iceland and farther south than the southernmost tip of Argentina. Unfortunately, there is little surviving evidence in the ship's papers of her cargoes and ports of call, except that the British Consul Agent in Lota, Chile did sign and stamp her papers on 10 July. Similarly, six days later the British Vice Consul in Valparaiso, also in Chile, carried out the same procedure. The *Pembroke Castle* departed Valparaiso three days later and headed for home, a long and arduous voyage.

The homeport for which they headed was Liverpool. They seemed to have made good progress, for in late November they were hugging the west coast of Ireland, but a few days before reaching their destination disaster struck. On the twenty-sixth of that month Benjamin was washed overboard and drowned. What a terrible disaster this was for a young man of only twenty-four, with such a bright future, a possible candidate to become master mariner, to be struck down so quickly and decisively. Exact details of the incident do not exist but in this part of the North Atlantic heavy seas, strong wind and storms are regular occurrences, and accidents of this nature were far too common. In stormy conditions thousands of gallons of seawater could be washed over the ship's deck in seconds, and with just one moment's lack of concentration you would be swept overboard.

The *Pembroke Castle* arrived in Liverpool three days later where Benjamin's death was reported to the authorities. Detective Superintendent I Farrier of the Liverpool Constabulary made an investigation of the incident and a short report was written in the ship's 'Agreement and Account of Crew' document. It read as follows:

"Liverpool 2nd Dec. 1885 - I have made inquiry respecting the death of the within named Benjamin Davies, Mate and find the evidence fully corroborates the entry in Office (ship's) Log Book. Signed I. Farrie"

When this news reached the family at Pantywylan it must have hit them like a bolt of lightning and broken his parents' hearts. Their eldest son, who had achieved so much in his young life and of whom they were immensely proud, had been taken from them. What a blow not only to his parents but also to the whole family and so difficult for them to come to terms with. Perhaps they never did, for as mentioned earlier both his parents, Frances and John, died just two and a half years later. Life at Pantywylan for the surviving children was never to be the same again, and must have felt empty without their parents. After this experience it's little wonder that the five remaining sons did not turn to the sea for their living.

Mary, the eldest daughter, was twenty-four years old when her parents died. She married Moylgrove blacksmith David Benjamin Davies, and they made their home in Glanawen, Moylgrove. They had seven children: Frances Sophia, Lizzie Anne, Mary Ellen, Benjamin Lodwig, John George, Leah Rosina, and David Clifford. Benjamin Lodwig became a congregational minister, John George an officer in the army, later becoming a commercial traveller in Carmarthen. Leah Rosina died in infancy and David Clifford followed in his father's footsteps, becoming a blacksmith.

Margaret was the second daughter and stayed on in Pantywylan, living there all of her life. In the immediate years after her parents' deaths she was needed to look after the younger members of the family. Three of these were under the age of 12 in 1888.

A photograph of six of the Pantywylan children. Front row: William, George and Evan. Back row: Leah, David and Margaret.

John, the eldest son, married Elizabeth Morris of Deinol farm near the village of Glynarthen in South Cardiganshire. By the mid 1890s John was farming in Dolgian Farm in the nearby village of Brongest. They had six daughters, the last two being twins, but sadly Elizabeth died soon after giving birth to them in 1902. In 1906 John married Mary Davies of Penpontbren Farm, also in the village of Glynarthen and lived in Blaenwaun Farm a short distance away. They had three children: twin boys Thomas Emrys and Evan George, and daughter Catherine Olwen.

Leah became a schoolteacher and eventually retired from the profession in 1930, having spent the previous twenty-five years as the head mistress of St Dogmaels' Infant School. She took a keen interest in the social welfare of the village. Among some of the organizations she was associated with were the Women's Institute and the National Savings Association, of which in 1917 she was the honorary secretary. In her final years her eyesight began to fail her and she was nearly blind when she died in 1955.

After leaving school **George Phillip** entered the drapery trade and was apprenticed at the New Manchester House drapery shop in Cardigan. He later moved on firstly to Swansea as an improver and afterwards to London. He was appointed representative of the Manchester firm of A & S Henry & Co. in South Wales and was considered the best commercial traveller in his area. He was also a religious man and was involved in many organizations both in Swansea where he made his home and in Cardigan after his retirement to Pantywylan. He was a member of the Executive Committee of the Cardigan and District Memorial Hospital. He died in 1938.

William Henry was twelve years old when his parents died in 1888. Twelve years later, in the 1901 census he was recorded as a twenty-four-year-old commercial traveller living at 3 Trinity Place, Swansea. It is not known in what business he worked or whether it was in any way connected to his brother George Phillip. William Henry in the first few years of the 1900's emigrated to Canada and in 1910 in Ontario married Delia Elizabeth Thomson, daughter of a Scottish Presbyterian dentist. His occupation at this time was manager of a Motor Wheel Company. In the following eight years they had three sons: John Marquis, George Evan and William Alexander. He died about 1945 and his descendants still live in Canada and America to this day.

Evan Griffith was born in 1879 and became a congregational minister studying at Brecon Theological College. After his ordination he ministered at churches in Gloucester, Bristol, London and Cardiff. He married Marie Bees from Bristol and they had two children, Megan and James Lodwig. He died aged 62 whilst visiting the old home of Pantywylan in 1941. He is buried in Moylgrove's St Peters Church graveyard.

David was the youngest of the Pantywylan family and was seven years old when his parents died in 1888. Margaret an older sister brought him up in Pantywylan. Like Margaret he lived and farmed Pantywylan all of his life and in 1939 died after a short illness , which necessitated an operation and a stay in Cardigan Hospital. He is remembered on his parent's memorial stone at St Peters Church graveyard.

There are three other very interesting members closely connected to this Pantywylan family and I include them in this section. The first of these is John Davies' father-in-law Benjamin Lodwig. He was born in 1802 in Moylgrove and was also brought up there. He certainly would have spent some of his childhood days at Ceibwr, the little beach about a mile from that village, where there was some shipping and trading activity at that time. An old Lime Kiln from those days still survives.

An example of a typical lime burning kiln used in this area, preserved in the village of Llangranog

Two ships waiting to be unloaded at Ceibwr Beach

This old photograph shows Ceibwr beach about a mile from the village of Moylgrove and only a few hundred yards from Pantywylan. The two little vessels were probably unloading limestone or culm (cwlwm). To the left of where the photographer stands there existed a Lime Kiln. Its remains can still be seen there today.

Benjamin spent almost all of his working life at sea, taking the Board of Trade examination to become a master mariner in 1851, although he had been a master of many vessels for twenty-six years before this. The usual application to apply for his Certificate of Service still survives but sadly not in good condition, and the section which records the names of the vessels that he sailed on has been torn off and lost. The information therefore regarding Benjamin's life at sea until 1851 is limited. It still gives some very useful information nevertheless. He began his seafaring life in 1818, serving four years apprenticeship on a Cardigan ship. He then served on two other vessels until 1825 when he became master of a 180-ton Bristol registered vessel, serving on her until 1827. In 1825 Benjamin married Leah Davies of Pantywylan. In May 1828 he bought eight of the sixty four shares in the newly built 37-ton Cardigan sloop *Susan Jane*, the remainder of the shares were bought by nine other investors, one of these being his brother-in-law, the previously mentioned Daniel Davies, Minister of Capel Mair. Benjamin was also the *Susan Jane's* master. A year later in May 1829 he sold four of these shares to a John Lodwig, probably his brother and also a master mariner. From that date John Lodwig became master of the ship. Benjamin held his remaining four shares until 1836 when he sold them to John Evans, merchant, of Cardigan.

From 1829 to 1841 he was master of the 84-ton Cardigan schooner *Cygnet*, a vessel involved in coastal trading only. A sample of her destined voyages as described in the Lloyds Registers during these years were -

Ship	Master	Year	Owner	Port	Voyages
Cygnet	B Lodwig	1832	Lodwig & Co	Cardigan	Newport coaster
"	"	1833	"	"	Liverpool coaster
"	"	1835	"	"	Gloucester to Newport
"	"	1840	"	"	Gloucester to Newry

From 1843 to 1851 he was the master of another Cardigan vessel, *Rose and Ellen*. Her voyages were a little farther afield and to ports in the Baltic Sea, Rouen, Hamburg, Antwerp and Dunkirk. In 1851 while under Benjamin's command the *Rose and Ellen* was driven onshore by strong winds near Holyhead, Anglesey and consequently broke up. Luckily Benjamin survived and about 1853 he became master of the previously mentioned Cardigan vessel *Agenoria*, a ship with a very similar trading pattern as the *Rose and Ellen*. Also as previously mentioned he was her master until about 1862, when his son-in-law John Davies took over as her master. Benjamin was then sixty years old, having been to sea for forty-four of them, thirty-six of these as a master mariner. You could say he had done his bit. One would imagine he would be ready to put his feet up, relax and tell tales of life at sea in the old days but no, Benjamin had a lot more to offer.

In 1865 a vacancy occurred at Cardigan Workhouse for the position of master of that establishment. Benjamin's name was put forward, being proposed by O Phillips Esq. and seconded by Mr

William Phillips. There were five other applicants and the method used to choose a suitable candidate was that members of the Board of Guardians in a series of elections would each vote for their individual preferred choice. The candidate with the least votes would withdraw. After a series of four elections and one voluntary withdrawal the six candidates were whittled down to the one successful candidate, our Benjamin Lodwig.

The work of a Master of the Workhouse was not an easy one by any means. The Board of Guardians were always anxious to keep the cost of running the workhouse as low as possible. The master had to account for every penny spent. For instance he had to be able to adequately feed and clothe the paupers on a very limited budget. There were many more responsibilities of course, such as arranging apprenticeships for suitable young men residing in the workhouse, usually with local craftsmen. As previously mentioned Benjamin in June 1865 arranged that David John Shepherd be apprenticed to his son-in-law John Davies, master of the ship *Agenoria*.

In 1869 the post of Master of the Cardigan Workhouse again came up for re-election, but Benjamin on this occasion failed to be re-elected. In 1871 he was living next door to his daughter Leah Rees in Langwm Street, St Dogmaels. Leah was one of three of his daughters who married master mariners. He died in 1886 aged eighty-three, being looked after in his final days at Pantywylan by his daughter and son-in-law Frances and John Davies.

The second 'outsider' I include here is Benjamin Lodwig's wife Leah Davies. She was born in 1803 on a farm situated approximately half a mile from Pantywylan called Penwern. Farming Penwern at that time were her parents John David and his wife Elizabeth. They had two sons, John and George.

John (the son) remained in Penwern, married, and raised a family of eight children, five boys and three girls. Of the five boys two became surgeons, one became minister of the gospel, one went to live in Swansea and one remained to farm Penwern.

The second son George married Elizabeth and moved the half-mile down the road to farm Pantywylan. George and Elizabeth did not have children of their own, although it seems that they would have liked to. George and Elizabeth adopted one of his brother John's three daughters and brought her up as their own at Pantywylan. The adopted daughter's name was Leah Davies and family folk law has it that after one Sunday evening service at Bethel Chapel Moylgrove George carried Leah all the way home to Pantywylan on his shoulders. From that Sunday evening Leah lived the rest of her life at Pantywylan as if she had been the natural daughter of George and Elizabeth, and of course went on to marry Benjamin Lodwig.

Daniel Davies Minister of the Gospel

The third and final of the three 'outsiders' is brother to the above Leah Davies, one of the five sons of John David of Penwern. He was Daniel Davies, who became minister of the gospel and the minister of Capel Mair Congregational Chapel, Cardigan. He became well known and much respected throughout the length and breadth of Wales, not only for his preaching but also for his work in furthering the cause of the Congregationalist movement at that time.

He was born in 1780 and as a young man was urged to start preaching by the then minister of Bethel Chapel, Moylgrove, the Rev. John Phillips. In 1809 he embarked on a preaching tour of north Wales and settled in the village of Rhes-y-cae, Flintshire where he was ordained. Within a few years he had returned to assist his old minister John Phillips at Bethel but soon there came a call for him to assist a new Congregational Chapel in Cardigan. This meant he had to give up his duties at Bethel. This new chapel at Cardigan was Capel Mair, situated in St Mary's Lane. The small congregation, mainly of poor women, had set about some years earlier to build a chapel, a rudimentary building, which they were unable to finish completely due to the lack of funds while also leaving themselves in debt.

Daniel worked hard touring the country on preaching tours and collecting money to pay off the debt on the building and to effect improvements to make the building useable. In 1831 when the old building had become too small and too shabby it was demolished and a much bigger one built on the same plot of land. He also kept a school for several years. In addition to Capel Mair he assisted the Congregational meetinghouse in Ty-Rhos near Cilgeran, succeeding in building a Chapel there. Similarly in St Dogmaels he was instrumental in the building of Capel Dogwel. So popular was the Rev. Daniel Davies that the service to mark his jubilee in 1864 had to be held outdoors due to the many hundreds that wanted to attend. During his time as minister of Capel Mair the congregation had increased from sixteen to 400.

What is not generally known about Daniel Davies is that he had a strong connection to seafaring. Daniel had financial interests in many of the ships that were built in and sailed from Cardigan. His name appears on many of the pages of the ship registration books of that port as the owner of shares of many vessels. The following are some of the ships of which he was a shareholder and the number of their shares he owned. All were registered in Cardigan :

Vessel	Date	Shares
Cygnet	January 1826	10
"	November 1829	18
Frances	May 1830	4
Susan Jane	June 1836	11
Valiant	September 1836	14
Rose and Ellen	January 1848	10
Agenoria	October 1852	8
"	April 1862	16

It was not uncommon in those days for vicars and non-conformist ministers to own shares in local ships but Daniel at times became even more involved. For instance, in 1863/64 he was recorded on the Crew List of the *Agenoria* as her managing owner. In 1863 he was eighty-three years old so whether he actually did manage the ship at that age or perhaps given the title as a mark of respect for the grand old man, we will never know. He seems to have led an incredibly energetic and enthusiastic life, so perhaps the former was the case. Daniel died in January 1867 having worked tirelessly and passionately all of his life for his faith and the Congregationalist movement, not only in Cardigan but also throughout Wales. The following report of his death was written in the Cardigan & Tivy-Side Advertiser:

"Death of the Rev. Daniel Davies: – It is with the deepest regret that we have to record the death of the above respected gentleman, which took place at his residence, Pendre, Cardigan, on Friday, 18th instant, at the advanced age of 87 years. He has been a faithful servant of the gospel for upwards of sixty years. He was ordained a minister in Flintshire, North Wales where he remained for about five years, and the coming to Cardigan about 54 years ago. On Wednesday the funeral took place, when a great number of people, almost every denomination, from all parts of the county, assembled to pay him their last tribute of respect. He was buried at the parish church of Verwig. Most of the respectable tradesmen of the town closed their respective places of business during the time of the funeral. Mr Davies was a person that was much respected by all that knew him and we believe that he had no single enemy."

He was buried with his wife Mary and their only daughter Elizabeth, wife of W W Lloyd, master of the schooner *Hibernia* of Cardigan.

Evan, John and Mary Davies' fifth child

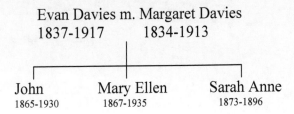

Evan Davies m. Margaret Davies
1837-1917   1834-1913

John   Mary Ellen   Sarah Anne
1865-1930   1867-1935   1873-1896

CHAPTER 5

Evan – the fifth child of John and Mary Davies

Evan was born in July 1837 and would have had the same experiences as his eldest brother John growing up in Panteg. He seems to have been as keen and enthusiastic as his brother in all seafaring matters, also becoming a master mariner, but his career steered a slightly different course. While John confined himself to his own business operating out of Cardigan and in 'Home Waters', Evan sailed further afield for ship owners from Cardigan, Aberystwyth, Liverpool and Swansea. They both became very experienced master mariners in their own right.

It was not known for certain on which vessel his brother John had began his sailing career; this was not the case for Evan. On his application to become a ship's mate some years later, he clearly states that he served four years of apprenticeship on his father's ship *Thetis*, beginning in August of 1849 at exactly twelve years old. This was a very young age for a boy to be starting his working life and unheard of in our modern times of course.

Alas, this was Victorian Britain when a much different attitude towards children and work existed. The typical Victorian approach to child labour was to send very young children down dark, wet coal mines or into dusty, noisy Lancastrian cotton mills. This was not the case here but I suspect it was done to continue his education and teach him a trade. It was to prove very successful; by the age of twenty-eight he had become a master mariner.

During the next eight years Evan's career followed the same pattern as many of the sailors in his family. Besides the *Thetis* he sailed on three other vessels, the first being the Cardigan registered *Friends,* a schooner of 85 tons, a very similar vessel to that of his father's and also employed in the coastal trade. After a short period of about seven months he returned once again to help his father on the *Thetis.* In June 1858 Evan signed on as able seaman on the Liverpool ship *Goliah*, a very different vessel to those he was used to.

The most obvious difference was her size, since the *Goliah* was, at 900 tons, at least ten times larger than the *Thetis*. Her voyages were different too; for the period Evan sailed on her, her destined voyage, as recorded in the Lloyds Registers, was from Liverpool to Bombay.

He served on this vessel for nearly ten months; probably time enough for one return voyage to Bombay and back. (Interestingly, the *Goliah* was later bought by Cardigan merchant Herbert Davies). Whether the experience of sailing to Bombay was good or bad, Evan took his time before going back to sea, and it was eighteen months before he signed on the *Magdelene* of Aberystwyth in September 1860. Perhaps this time away from the sea was spent studying at a Navigation School. In those days the *Magdelene* did most of her sailing from Liverpool across the Bay of Biscay to ports on the Spanish peninsular. Evan signed off this ship in May 1861.

If Evan had indeed attended a Navigational School it had been a wise decision, for three months later on 15 August he sat the examination at the port of Dublin to become a ships mate and was successful. The following are the words written on the certificate of competency issued to him by the Board of Trade:

"It has been reported to us that you have been found duly qualified to fulfil the duties of Mate in the Merchant Service we do hereby in pursuance of the Merchant Shipping Act of 1854 grant you this Certificate."

He returned once again to Cardigan to find his next vessel, the *Europa*. She was Cardigan built, Cardigan owned and Cardigan registered, a true 'Cardi' you might say. The *Europa* was a brig, a two-masted vessel with square sails on both masts, suitable for deep-sea sailing and one of the largest to be built on the banks of the River Tivy at 155 tons. Her owners were Williams & Co.

Evan joined her crew as mate in November 1861 and during the ten months or so of his service on board, Swansea was her centre of operations, trading between there and ports in the Mediterranean sea. It's not certain what kind of cargo the *Europa* carried in those days but the Port Books record her arrival in Swansea from Alicante on 19 June 1863 with a cargo of silver ore for Dillwyn & Co. I dare say she carried similar cargoes when Evan was her mate.

During the following four years or so he was employed as mate in the following vessels, building up valuable experience for his future:

- *Tirsah,* a schooner owned by R. Richards & Co. of Aberystwyth, trading in the Mediterranean.
- *Mary Elizabeth,* a brig registered in Newport, Monmouthshire, trading in South America.
- *Wish,* a brig registered in Plymouth, trading in the West Indies and Mediterranean.
- *Alma,* a barque registered in the Prince Edward Islands, Canada trading between Swansea, the Mediterranean, and Prince Edward Island.

Evan was a very busy mariner at this time, seemingly always at sea, but he did find time to return home to St Dogmaels on some occasions. In the spring of 1864 he married Margaret Davies, a shopkeeper's daughter. Margaret and her father lived in Mount Pleasant, Moylgrove, where the young couple settled to raise a family and remained there until their deaths.

What better reason could a young man have to try to advance his career than a wife and the prospect of a family? This may have been the encouragement, if he needed any, for Evan to apply for and then to sit the examination to become master mariner at the port of Dublin in February 1865. Again he was successful. His first ship as master was the 196-ton brigantine *Edith May,* built and registered on Prince Edward Island and like the above mentioned *Alma* owned by William Richards, trading mainly out of Swansea. Evan went on to have a long association with William Richards, his brother Thomas and their Prince Edward Island built ships.

It must have been a daunting experience for him on 28 September 1865 in Swansea, not only was it his first day of joining the ship but also his first day as master. He had a great deal going for him though, with his experience both as a sailor and a mate. As a rule of thumb, the mate is responsible for the smooth running and sailing of the ship on a day-to-day basis and the master makes the big decisions as and when necessary. He also had the advantage of previously having sailed to the Mediterranean. *Edith May's* destinations while he was her master were, in the order visited; Swansea – Vigo, Spain – Seville, Spain – Newcastle-on-Tyne – Cagliari, Italy – Llanelli, Wales.

He signed off on 3 August 1866 in Llanelli. Again it's not certain what cargo the *Edith May* carried during Evans time as her master, but in August of the following year, 1867, the Cambrian News reports her arrival in Swansea from Buctonche, New Brunswick with a cargo of timber for Richards, Power & Co. In April 1868 she arrived in Swansea with a cargo of zinc ore from Carloforte, Sardinia. This kind of trading was typical of the Richards' ships at that time.

William Richards himself was born in Swansea and went to sea, became a master mariner, ship owner and ship builder. He owned shipyards on Prince Edward Island, Canada where all his ships were built. The majority of these were transferred back to the UK; many were employed in the Swansea copper trade. William's brother Thomas Picton Richards was his agent in Swansea.

It was cheaper to build wooden ships in Canada where there was an abundant supply of timber rather than transport the timber home to the UK and build them here. William was one of many who built wooden ships on the east coast of Canada at that time; this competition was sometimes blamed for the early demise of ship building in the small ports of West Wales such as Cardigan and New Quay, although the end was inevitable once steam and steel became the norm in shipbuilding.

As was the pattern of things to come, Evans' next ship as master was also a Prince Edward Island built, William Richards owned and Swansea operated brig. She was the 274-ton *Grace* and the following lists the destinations visited between September 1867 and January 1869, viz.: Swansea, Wales - Tunis, Tunisia - Cagliari, Italy - Lisbon, Portugal – Llanelli, Wales - St Johns, Newfoundland - Tilt Cove, Newfoundland – Swansea, Wales – Oran, Algeria – Carloforte, Italy – Swansea, Wales. This confirms the similarity in the pattern of trading of *Grace* and the *Edith May*.

These vessels were almost entirely deployed in supplying copper and other metal ores to the smelting factories in the Swansea valley and importing timber from Canada. Again, the Cambrian News in September 1866 reports the *Grace* arriving in Swansea with a cargo of timber from Shadiac, Newfoundland and in August 1869 from Tilt Cove, Newfoundland with 456 tons of copper and nickel ore for Thomas Bennett.

As was becoming the norm, Evan's next ship was also another Richards' ship built on Prince Edward Island. She was the 192-ton brig *Nimble,* trading out of Swansea into the Mediterranean and Canada with similar cargoes. While on her voyage between Pound Harbour, Newfoundland, and Swansea and in the position of 51.47 North 33.44 West, mid way between Canada and Ireland, a tragic accident was reported in the ship's log.

Twenty-one-year-old boatswain Thomas Phillips, a Cardigan man, fell overboard and drowned. This kind of accident was far too common in those days of sail. In fact four years later, not on Evan's watch this time, another crew member, fifteen-year-old apprentice William Watts, also fell overboard this ship and drowned. The safety standards of those days were not a reflection on the masters or any members of the crew; it's just how things were at the time. Health and Safety Officers had not been created in 1869; thank goodness things have improved today. The *Nimble* arrived in Swansea on 16 November with 500 tons of copper ore for H Bath & Son.

The *One* was Evan's next ship and the first on which he was to venture into the southern oceans and the South Americas as a master. The *One* was a 523-ton barque also Richards owned and Prince Edward Island built and registered in Swansea. They departed the port of

Swansea on 5 December 1870 and arrived in Rio de Janeiro on 23 January 1871, where they stayed for almost one month to discharge and load cargo. They set sail once again, this time towards the north and their next destinations of Argab, Denmark; Dieppe, Netherlands; Middlesbrough and then Hartlepool. While in Hartlepool Evan met with the problem of desertion by some members of his crew and writes the following in the Captain's Log:

"20th December 1871 Hartlepool - I within certify that Thomas Shapter, William Robert Jenkinson and Robert Stevenson have refused to go on board after I had agree with coachman to take them a board they run away. I had to pay the coachman 15 shillings which I shall decut out of their wages. On the same day I had to give my men in charge of the police, which have gather the five men before the magistrate at 11.a.m. on the 21st. They all then agree to go on-board the ship. The Magistrate orders me to pay the expenses, which were 17 shillings, and to be deducted out of the wages of the said five men. Signed Evan Davies Master"

The problem of desertion was ever present it seemed no matter what port in the world a ship visited. Were these men discontent with their lot aboard the *One*, were they having such a good time in the pubs and inns of Hartlepool or was it that they couldn't face up to another long voyage to South America? Evan must have resolved the crew problem, for the very next day that long voyage began. They set sail once again to their first port of call of Valparaiso in Chile, known even today for its copper ore deposits.

Most Swansea ships involved in that trade would have visited this port at some time. Every 'Cape Horner', a term referring to captains of sailing ships that had regularly made the voyage around Cape Horn, would also have visited Valparaiso at least once in his career. The *One* visited two other Chilean ports on that voyage, Mollendo and Maxillones, before returning to Hamburg, Germany.

After a mere twelve days Evan and his crew turned the ship around and before heading south to Chile once again called into Cardiff, presumably to load a cargo of coal and perhaps to receive orders. While in Cardiff, however, eight members of her crew deserted and, not surprisingly, eight new members were recruited on the same day, 28 December 1872. A few days later they headed south to their destination Iquique in Chile, also a copper ore-mining region. They arrived there on 26 May 1873. Whilst in this port the ship's apprentice James Furlong completed his apprenticeship and the British Vice-Consul at Iquique sanctioned that he be re-engaged as able seaman. With her cargo loaded they began their return voyage on 6 August to Leith, Scotland arriving there on 2 December 1873 having taken practically four months to do so. I'm sure they all took quite some time to find their land legs.

After all this time at sea Evan deserved a long break. His movements for the next twenty months are unclear apart from the fact that he was the master of the *St Laurence*, another of William Richards' barques, at some time during 1874. There are little details of that voyage surviving. In the Lloyd's Registers for the previous year 18/2/3 it is recorded that her destined voyage was Swansea to Prince Edward Island.

It is probably safe to say that Evan did go home at this time, as he always had done in between some of his voyages at sea. As a result of course he had now a growing family at home in Mount Pleasant. There to meet him would have been Margaret his wife, his eight-year-old son John and six-year-old daughter Mary Ellen. A second daughter Sarah Anne was born in 1873.

By August of 1875 Evan was back at sea as master of the ship *Evangeline*, another of the Swansea copper barques owned by Richards, Power & Co. The Richards in this case was Thomas Picton Richards. Evan remained her master until at least 1882 and probably beyond that. Her destinations during this time were from ports in Europe and South Wales to South and North America, i.e. Rotterdam, Calais, Rouen, Bordeaux, Cardiff, Newport, Penarth, sailing to ports in Peru, Chile, Uruguay, New Orleans, Baltimore, and Bermuda.

Evan had by now rounded the dangerous Cape Horn many times, a route sometimes called 'Sailors Graveyard' because of the many lives lost and ships perished due to its strong winds, difficult currents and large waves. He would now certainly qualify as a true 'Cape Horner'. Some of these voyages have been described in the earlier accounts of his two nephews, William Evans and Benjamin Davies, therefore I shall be brief. In general, Evan's time as the master of the *Evangeline* appeared to go as well as you would expect of any experienced master, though it would never have been easy for him.

Evan did sail on beyond 1882 and in the census returns of 1891 he was not at home in Mount Pleasant with his family. He was quite probably still at sea, but ten years later, the 1901 census records that he was at home, a sixty-three-year-old retired master mariner. After well over forty years at sea he had cut his ties with Swansea, ships, masts, sails, crews, cargoes, the Richards brothers and even the sea itself to hang up his trusty sextant and compass and retire.

It had been a long journey since he joined his father's *Thetis* at the age of twelve. He himself had become one of the old master mariners who knew sail and sailing ships and who were soon to become a dying breed. He spent his last years settled down with Margaret in Mount Pleasant, where the community around him held him in high regard and great respect. After all that time apart, they both deserved to spend some peaceful years to enjoy each other's company.

They lived in Mount Pleasant until both of their deaths, Evan in 1917 of gastritis and tyncope (hardening of the arteries) and Margaret four years earlier in 1913. The informant recording Evans' death at Cardigan Registrar Office was his nephew David Davies of Pantywylan. His obituary was recorded in the Cardigan Tivyside Advertiser:

"Obituary: The death took place on Friday of last week of Capt. Evan Davies, Mount Pleasant, at the advanced age of 80. The deceased had retired from seafaring life many years ago, having sailed many times round the "Horn", and visited the different ports in Europe. The funeral was a large and representative one, which testified to the respect in which the deceased was held."

Evan and Margaret's children

Evans and Margaret's son John Davies –
Rural Dean

Evan and Margaret had three children; the eldest was **John**, born in 1865. In 1886 he entered St Bees Theological College, Cumbria. He became a deacon in 1889 and a priest in 1891, both in the City of Worcester, and a curate in the hamlet of Hill, Warwickshire. From there he moved back to Wales and was the Vicar of Neath, St John-juxta-Swansea, Penbrey and Llandyry, Llanrhidian and Penclawdd. He became Rural Dean of West Glamorgan in the Diocese of Swansea and Brecon in 1918, an achievement his parents would surely have been proud to witness had they lived to see that day. John himself died in 1930 at the Victoria Nursing Home, Bournemouth.

Mary Ellen their first daughter was born in 1867 and died in 1935.

Sarah Anne was born in 1873 and became a schoolteacher but unfortunately died at the young age of twenty-three years.

Eleanor, John and Mary Davies' sixth child

Eleanor Davies m. George Owens
1839-1878   1837-1905

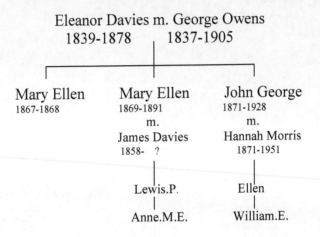

Mary Ellen	Mary Ellen	John George
1867-1868	1869-1891	1871-1928
	m.	m.
	James Davies	Hannah Morris
	1858- ?	1871-1951
	Lewis.P.	Ellen
	Anne.M.E.	William.E.

CHAPTER 6

Eleanor – the sixth of John and Mary Davies children

Eleanor, or Ellen, as most records that exist of her life refer to her, was born in 1839. Like her brothers and sisters she was brought up in Panteg, living there until she was twenty-six years old, when the inevitable happened and she married a mariner. Ellen's mariner was twenty-eight-year old George Owens of the 'White Lion' Public House, Aberporth and he too came from a seafaring family. They were married by the Rev. Daniel Davies in Hope Chapel, an English Congregational Chapel situated in the Strand, Cardigan, on 28 March 1865. George Owens was already a master mariner, as was his father John Owens (originally from Llangranog).

Naturally Ellen Davies had now become Ellen Owens and as previously mentioned her father John purchased an 18-ton smack about this time and named her *Ellen Owens*. I suspect that there was a strong connection between the events! It seems that they first set up home in St Dogmaels as their three children were born there. On 14 December 1867 their first, Mary Ellen was born, but sadly, as was often the case for children in those days, she died in infancy.

A year later on 29 January 1869 a second daughter was born and she too was named Mary Ellen. In 1871 their only son John George was born.

All the families I have described previously had one thing in common; their lives and work were almost exclusively linked with the sea and seafaring. This Owens family was no exception. In addition to this they were landlords of the 'White Lion' Public House in Aberporth.

Through most of the 1800s this village was noted as an important centre of fishing, salting and smoking of herring, but there is no evidence this Owens family were involved in this activity.

Many of Aberporth's inhabitants of the day were also known to have owned or held shares in small sailing vessels. The Owens' were no exception. They also sailed and managed their own vessels. George's father John, as previously mentioned, was born in Llangranog, a small seaside village some four miles north of Aberporth and known for producing first class sailors. His wife Mary was born in Nevern. They probably settled in the village of Aberporth some time in the early 1820s, for at least six of their seven children were born there.

It's unknown when exactly they took over at 'White Lion', most likely well before 1841, as they then lived in the area of Aberporth called Bank y Dyffryn where the Public House is situated. John and Mary were a pretty astute couple it seems and used the 'White Lion' to supplement their income if their seafaring business ever took a downturn or when their ships were laying up for the winter on the River Tivy at Cardigan.

The Registration and Transaction Books of ships registered in the port of Cardigan show that in 1837 John Owens owned twenty shares and was the principal owner of the vessel *Active* of Cardigan. The remainder of her sixty-four shares was held by a shipwright, a sail maker, a widow, and six local farmers. Built in 1826 this vessel was a single-masted sloop of twenty-six tons burthen. She was ideally suited for the local coastal trades, being able to sail onto creeks and beaches at high tide, wait for the tide to recede and comfortably sit on the sand while unloading her cargo before sailing out again on the next tide.

The cargo would usually consist of coal or culm from such places as Llanelli and Pembray or limestone from Pembroke and Lydstep. This was the kind of trade the Owens family was involved in. On August 30 1847 the *Active* was on one such voyage, this time returning home to Aberporth from Swansea. While negotiating the dangerous narrow stretch of water called Ramsey Sound, situated between Ramsey Island and the Pembrokeshire coast near St David's, the little vessel ran into trouble and sank with the loss of all hands.

Usually, this kind of vessel would have two or three crew members but it is not known the number on that day. We do know that two of the sailors who perished were twenty-six-year-old David Owens and his fourteen-year-old brother John. Both were John and Mary Owens' sons. This was a very sad day indeed for the family at the White Lion and the community of Aberporth. This disaster is recorded on the Owens' family gravestone at Blaenporth Parish Church.

While a sailor's life was tough and dangerous, the loss of life heart-breaking for families and their communities, there was one other consideration to take into account and that was the loss of the ship. If she were not insured, as many ships weren't in those days, shareholders lost every penny that was invested.

It was also about 1837 that John Owens invested in the newly-built Cardigan vessel *Mary*. This ship was similar in practically every way to the above *Active,* being a single-masted sloop of 23-tons built to manage the same kind of coastal trade around the lower Cardiganshire and Pembrokeshire coasts. The cargoes she carried and destinations she visited were also very similar. John Owens at purchase acquired sixteen of the *Mary's* shares and was joint principal owner with James James, a shipwright (possibly the builder of the vessel). Other shareholders were a mariner, rope maker, sail maker, ironmonger, miller and a yeoman. John Owens became the principal owner when James James sold a number of his shares to a Cardigan banker, John Evans.

This is how the position remained until early 1855 when on 14 February of that year sixty-six-year-old John died. John had appointed James Owens (probably a relative), late of the Wig, Llangranog, to be the Executor of his will and also left him four of the *Mary's* shares. The remainder of his sixteen shares were bequeathed to his wife Mary. Within a matter of two months Mary had acquired by bill of sale not only the above four shares from James Owens but also a further sixteen shares from the above-mentioned banker John Evans. She was now the principal owner.

Mary was not a woman to sit back and let the men run the business on her behalf but took the lead herself and was the *Mary's* managing owner for the remaining years of this little vessel's life. I suspect this lady had the strength of character to manage without any problems whatsoever; after all she and her husband had been in the business a long time, not forgetting either the qualities required of a landlady of a public house. It was quite usual for vessels such as this to only sail from spring to autumn, primarily to avoid the worst of the winter weather around the dangerous Pembrokeshire coastline.

For example, for the period from 1 July to 6 November 1866 the *Mary* made seven voyages between Milford, Aberporth, and Cardigan and thereafter was laid up on the River Tivy at Cardigan for the remainder of the winter. In 1869 *Mary's* master was forty-seven-year-old Thomas Humphreys of Aberporth and he employed one other crew member, his eighteen year old son John. The very first voyage of this year began on 1 April and was to Llanelli for a cargo of culm, which was delivered to Aberporth on the 21 of the month; in fact all her cargoes up to 13 July were delivered to Aberporth. They included eight loads of limestone from Milford and another of culm from Nolton.

These were typical of *Mary's* working life, bringing coal, culm and limestone from Pembrokeshire to Aberporth, Tresaith, Llangranog and Cardigan. These little ships, of which there were hundreds operating around the coast of Wales in the 1800's, could be considered as real workhorses, no doubt making a decent living for their owners and shareholders. Mary Owens' occupation recorded in the 1871 census shows that she was not only the landlady of the 'White Hart' but also a coal merchant. She was seventy-four years old at that time.

The owners of ships were obliged by law to deliver half-yearly the 'Account of Voyages and Crew' of vessels at their port of registration. Unfortunately in December 1873 this document was not handed in for another of the Owens ships, the *Mary Ellen*. Their son George Owens did deliver this document in February 1874 on behalf of his mother, who was this vessel's managing owner. Included with the document delivered to the shipping master at the Customs House in Cardigan was a letter of apology for this oversight, pointing out it was due to the serious illness of his mother. This grand old lady of the 'White Lion' was feeling the effects of a lifetime of hard work no doubt. Unfortunately life's trials and tribulations were not over for Mary yet. More disappointment was just around the corner.

The *Mary's* master and mate for 1874 were twenty-six year-old David and Morgan Jones from Pembryn. The *Mary* was put to work in the usual way during the first half of the year i.e. to Croft and Pembroke for limestone and to Hook and Penbrey for culm and coal, which were unloaded on the beaches of Aberporth, Tresaith and Llangranog. She discharged her cargo at Llangranog on 16 July and an entry written in her half yearly 'Account of Voyages and Crew' best describes what happened next:

"Master and Mate drowned 23rd July 1874 near St Anns Head. - The 'Mary' was no doubt run down by the steamer Milford of Milford about 23 July 1874 about midnight. The body of the Master David Jones was found off Milford some time after the collision." (The Milford was a Great Western Railway Steamer - presumably the body of Morgan Jones was never found).

This news must have come as a particularly hard blow to Mary. Apart from the loss of life of her crew, she had lost something that must have seemed like an affectionate friend by now. This little sloop had been in the family a very long time. It had been her husband's to begin with and she herself had looked after her ever since his death nearly twenty years earlier. It must have been a really hard blow for Mary. Two years later in June 1876 she herself died. She was buried with her husband John in Blaenporth Parish Church graveyard.

The death of the two Marys (George's mother and the ship) did not bring this particular Owens family's association with the sea to an end however. In 1866 George, approximately one year after his marriage to Ellen Davies at Cardigan bought a ship in his own right. She was the 29-ton schooner *Mary Ellen*, built at Milford. Her registered owner from that year was Owens & Co. and she was described as a Cardigan coaster. As verified in the Lloyds Registers, for much of the time that Owens & Co. was the owner of this vessel, George was her master. On the night 3 April 1871, the date the census was taken for that year, he was recorded as master of the *Mary Ellen* in the port of Hubberston Pill, Milford with two crew members David Rees and David Edwards, both from St Dogmaels.

It's not certain whether George had taken his family back to live permanently to Aberporth, at least not until around the time of his mother's death, when it appears that George and Ellen then took over as Licensees of the 'White Lion'. In May 1878 George was listed as a ship owner of the White Lion, Aberporth, one of the eleven directors of the Aberporth Mutual Ship Insurance Society Ltd.

By the following year the Company's papers show that his name had been withdrawn and the following might have been the reason. George and Ellen were now the Licensees of the White Lion, but sadly that situation did not last too long. In August of 1878 another very distressing event occurred which changed everything for George and the children, when Ellen, wife and mother, died suddenly of septicaemia. This Owens family had certainly gone through hardship in just a few years.

What was to happen to the children? As a mariner George was always at sea and men rarely, if ever, in those days stayed at home to look after their children. A solution was found, as they were taken in by their mother's family in St Dogmaels. The 1881 census shows Mary Ellen was a twelve-year-old schoolgirl living with her grandfather John Davies in High Street, St Dogmaels, probably in the 'Sailors Home' public house. Ten-year-old John George was living with his aunt Mary in the 'White Hart' public house, also in St Dogmaels. George himself, by 1891, had moved and was living with his married sister Margaret Humphreys at New Road, Aberporth.

This family's long association with the 'White Lion' had ended. The *Mary Ellen* was sold in 1880 to John Owen of Pentre Arms, Llangranog. Perhaps, in the end, it had all been too much for George, for he later moved to live in Cardiff and in 1905 died of senile decay at the age of sixty-four.

Ellen and George's children

John George became a Merchant's Clerk and worked for the Cardigan Mercantile Company, he married Hannah Morris in 1902 and they lived at Quay St., Cardigan. He was a Deacon at Capel Degwel, St Dogmaels. They had a daughter Ellen born in 1904 and a son, William Elwyn in 1910.

Mary Ellen, like her mother and of course many of the women in this family, found herself a mariner, whom she married at Cardiff Registry Office in July 1888, ten years after her mother's death. He was James Davies, a twenty-nine-year-old from Llanarth, a village a couple of miles inland from New Quay, Cardiganshire. James was the son of Griffith Davies, a shoemaker and landlord of the 'Rose Hall Arms' public house in that village.

By the time he married Mary Ellen, James Davies was an experienced sailor. He had gone to sea at about fifteen years of age as an apprentice on the New Quay built and registered ship *Cambria,* a barque of 233-tons, which operated in the Foreign Trade. In 1873-4 she sailed out of London for her New Quay owners Thomas & Co. In 1875, his apprenticeship completed, he sailed as an able seaman at first on two Aberystwyth vessels, the *Utopia* and *Glendovey,* and later on other vessels that were registered in ports such as London and Liverpool.

In 1880 he becomes a second mate of square-rigged sailing ships, taking his examination in the port of Hull. In 1882 he became a first mate in London. In 1883-4 he served on the Spanish owned *Olano.* This vessel was wrecked during that year. Fortunately for James he survived and in 1888, the year he married, he sailed as second mate on the *SS Dowlais,* registered in Cardiff and owned by the Dowlais Steam Ship Company. They had their roots in the production of iron and steel in Merthyr Tydfil.

After the wedding Mary Ellen and James lived in St Dogmaels and had two children, Lewis Picton in February 1890 and Annie Mary Ellen in September 1891. Once again disaster struck this family for Mary Ellen died just twenty days after giving birth to her daughter

Anne Mary Ellen. This was history repeating itself, but this time it was an even worst situation for their father James than it had been for his father-in-law George some thirteen years earlier. His children were so much younger, so young in fact that it would not have been possible for them to even remember their mother in later life. Good fortune really did not follow this Owens family.

A similar solution was found for the children Lewis Picton and Annie Mary Ellen as had been found for their mother and Uncle John George. A member of the Davies family in St Dogmaels looked after them. This particular member was their Great Aunty Anne, their grandmother's sister, and her husband Lewis Davies who lived in a small farm on the edge of the village called Penrallt-y-dre. Anne and Lewis had been married for some twenty-two years but did not have children. They brought the two children up as their own.

After Mary Ellen's death James eventually gave up the sea and moved to the Merthyr Tydfil area where he had family connections. He remarried and had one other child but he did support his children Annie Mary Ellen and Lewis Picton financially until they became of age, making regular visits to St Dogmaels to see them.

Lewis Picton as per this family's tradition also went to sea, beginning his seafaring life in 1907 at the port of Liverpool. He was seventeen years old when he began his apprenticeship on the Naiad, a large sailing vessel of 1787-tons. His forefathers would have been proud of him. He served out his apprenticeship on this ship but it was inevitable that Lewis would eventually move on to steam, as at this time it really was the end of sailing ships in the commercial world. Between 1911 and 1914 he sailed on a total of six steam ships, three as an able seaman and the others as third mate. They were:

Ship	Official No.	Tons	Owners
SS *Trevesso*	104678	2295	The Hein SS Co.
SS *Tregurno*	122660	2646	The Hein SS Co.
SS *Manchester City*	108835	2992	Manchester Liners Ltd

SS *Bretwalda*	129771	2586	Hall Bros. SS Co.
SS *La Blanca*	124026	6813	Argentine Cargo Lines
SS *Zingara*	110022	2214	Charles E Brightman & William H Turner

In January 1915 the age of steam ships was well established, but surprisingly he applied to be examined as a second mate on square-rigged sailing ships in the port of Swansea. Some of the details about him on the application form were: address - 23 Neville Street, Canton, Cardiff; the fact he had failed a previous examination due to his sight; that he was five feet eight inches tall, had grey eyes, brown hair, fair complexion and a tattoo on the back of his right hand. On this, his second attempt, surprisingly he didn't seem to have any problems with the examination, passing all categories: vision, colour vision, navigation, and seamanship.

The Clouds of War were Looming

By now the First World War had been under way for six months, but no one quite realised what was to come, especially the severe pounding the British Merchant fleet was to suffer in the following four years by enemy actions. Lewis in fact sailed throughout the war and came out safe on the other side although on at least one occasion only by the skin of his teeth. The ships he served on from 1914 to 1918 were owned by one London Company: Charles E. Brightman & William H. Turner. There were other subsidiary companies attached to this company, one being 'Z' Steamship Co. Ltd, and all their ships' names began with the letter Z. They had fifteen or so ships in their fleet; half were fitted with refrigerated holds and used for the Argentine meat trade; the remainder were used mainly on the Mediterranean and Black Sea routes.

The company's vessels that Lewis served were: *Zingara*, *Zeno*, *Zamora*, *Zermatt* and *Zinal*. Some of their destinations were: River Plate (Argentina), Campana (Argentina), and White Sea (North West Coast of Russia). Due to the war effort these vessels were also under the command of the Admiralty a great deal of this time.

All British and Allied Merchant Shipping during the First World War was in constant danger at sea with the threat of being torpedoed by German U-boats at any moment. This is what happened to the SS *Zermatt* when Lewis was her second mate. The SS *Zermatt* was sailing in the Atlantic on a voyage from Barry in South Wales with a cargo of coal for Campana, when on 24 July 1917 she was torpedoed by German U-boat 46 and sunk.

All but three crew members were saved; Lewis was amongst the survivors. Three months later he was once again back at sea on SS *War Penguin*[1] and then SS *Etha Rickmers*. From 1920 until 1924 he served on the ship SS *Final*.

In December 1920 Lewis married Mary Thomas, daughter of James Thomas ironmonger of Cardigan, at Tyrhos Chapel, Cilgeran. Lewis continued his career at sea but during the Great Depression of the 1930s he found it very difficult to find regular work, a consequence of the substantial reduction of international trade. Merchant ships were laid up in their hundreds in ports and estuaries around the world.

For unemployed sailors this meant a daily visit to the docks, in Lewis' case Cardiff, in the hope that one or other of the shipping agents would choose them for the next available voyage. Little is known of his seafaring life after this period. Lewis and Mary lived most of their married life in Cardiff when in 1974 he died a frail old man of eighty-four in Cardigan hospital. He was buried in the public cemetery in Cardigan.

Annie Mary Ellen married thirty-year-old David Thomas James, a mariner born in St Dogmaels, although his family's roots were in Llangranog and New Quay. The young couple did have one or two things in common; they both came from seafaring families and both their mothers died when they were very young. It was after their mothers' deaths that their young lives took very different courses.

1   *During the Great War years The British Government began an emergency shipbuilding program to replace the high number of ships lost, and decided for simplicity's sake to standardize their designs as far as possible. Orders were placed not only with ship builders in the UK but also in countries such as the US, Canada, Japan and Hong Kong. All these new vessels were given a name with the prefix 'War', e.g. War Penguin.*

Annie Mary Ellen at Aberporth beach

David Thomas James' grandfather Joshua James was originally from Llangranog. He married Margaret Evans, a widow, in 1848 and they lived in New Quay. Joshua lost his life during the night of the great storm of 25 October 1859 whilst sailing around the Pembrokeshire coast. That night winds were blowing from the North-North-West at gale force twelve. His ship *Mathildis* was lost off Dinas Head and all her crew perished. This famous storm is now generally known as the Royal Charter Storm.[2] Joshua was the only one of the New Quay's masters to have lost his life during that terrible night.

Joshua's stepson, John Evans, was also a crew member of the *Mathildis*, making it a disastrous night for his mother Margaret at home in New Quay. Margaret bore Joshua three sons, the last being James Thomas James in March 1858. He followed in his father's footsteps and went to sea at fourteen years old, joining the Aberystwyth schooner *Ellen Anne* as a boy on 9 February 1872. In the following seventeen years one could describe him as a prolific sailor, serving on no less than twenty-nine different ships.

During this period he served as an ordinary seaman, able seaman, boatswain, second and first mate. It could be considered he was an experienced sailor when he applied to take the examination

2 *The terrible storm that occurred in October 1859 was named The Royal Charter Storm after the ship 'Royal Charter' who on her voyage from Melbourne Australia to Liverpool, had been driven onto the north west coast of Anglesey and in spite of the best efforts of the crew and men on the shore 454 lives were lost, only twenty eight surviving. It was a terrible tragedy which gained even more notoriety due to the fact that many of these passengers were returning home rich with gold dug from the Australian gold fields.*

to become a second mate in Swansea in November 1889. As per usual on the application form some personal information is recorded about him. He was five feet four and a half inches tall with black hair, dark complexion, blue eyes, and with a cross tattooed on his left arm.

The last of the twenty-nine vessels he served on before his examination was the 1267-ton SS *Bempton* of London. James was on board on 16 August 1889 when the SS *Bempton*, under the command of Capt. David Evans. They left the port of Ibrail on the river Danube in Eastern Romania with a cargo of grain, barley, and flour for Antwerp. On the 28th of that month at 9.30 p.m. as they were approaching the port of Lisbon, Portugal the following happened:

"The weather being slightly hazy the Espichel Lighthouse was spotted and it was ascertained that they were on the correct course as was set by the master. At 2.10 a.m. dense fog set in and the engines were eased to dead slow at about 3 knots per hour, the whistle was sounded and the course altered to N. 1/4W Magnetic.

After going slow for about five to eight minutes, fishing boats were seen on the port bow lying at anchor or at their nets. The whistles of steamers were heard on the starboard bow and one astern. These steamers were probably passing in and out of the Tagus. The echo of the 'Bempton's whistle was about this time heard from the land, the helm was put hard-a-starboard to take the ship off the land, and the engines were put full speed astern. Land showed up at the same time, and at about 2.25 a.m. the vessel struck and remained fast.

On sounding the bells, water was found in the collision compartment and the chain locker. The engine-room and deck pumps were set going, but the water rapidly gained upon them, and the deck pumps became choked. The chain locker cover was put on and secured to keep the water from flowing over into the holds. At 3.30 a.m. the fog lifted a little, light from the Guia Lighthouse was seen, and it was found that the vessel was stranded about a quarter of a mile to the westward of that light.

A kedge was run out, but the vessel remained fast; and at 4 a.m. a boat was sent to communicate with the shore, but the men were not then allowed to land, not having pratique. At 5 a.m. a telegram was sent to Lloyd's agent at Lisbon for lighters and pumps, and at noon the lighters came alongside and the crew commenced to discharge the cargo; altogether about 500 tons being salved before the vessel was abandoned.

During the day No.1 hold was found to be full of water, while No.2 hold had 12ft. of water in it. On the following day pumps arrived from Lisbon, but were found to be in bad condition, and they would not work. On the 6th of September the vessel was abandoned, being full of water, and the crew were taken to Lisbon, and ultimately returned to the United Kingdom."

The above is an extract from the Board of Trade inquiry into the incident; the conclusion being amongst other things was that various changes in courses made after the visibility deteriorated were not right and proper. No allowances for the strong spring flood tide were made and the total neglect of the use of the lead was unjustified. The master alone was found to be in default and his certificate was suspended for three months. The master and crew had had a narrow escape, but things could have been much worse.

If James Thomas James had gone straight home to St Dogmaels when he arrived back in the UK he would have gone to Glantivon, the house where his wife and daughter lived. James had married Frances Sophia Phillips in May 1886 and they had, so far, two children. The first, Evan, died one month after his birth and Margaret Ellen was born the following year. Another son, David Thomas was born in June 1890 and another daughter, Frances Sophia, in March 1891. This was when the tide of good fortune once again turned against this small family in Glentivon.

It was during or shortly after giving birth to Frances Sophia that her mother died. Initially, I suspect, her sixty-nine-year-old widowed mother Eleanor, who also lived with them in Glantivon, looked after the children. Eighteen months later the situation turned worse for these three young children. On 31 October 1893 the Admissions and Discharge book of the Cardigan Workhouse in St Dogmaels shows that all three children were admitted to that institution before dinner on that day. The harsh conditions in these old Victorian workhouses are well recorded of course and there's nothing to suggest that it was any different in Cardigan. Little Frances Sophia only survived there for eighteen months before she died in February 1894 aged three years. Her older sister Margaret Ellen was discharged by order of the Board of Guardians in 1898 and at eleven years old was sent into service on Ffynongrog Farm, Mwnt near Cardigan.

Young David Thomas remained there until March 1903 and in the words of the Discharge page of the book, 'he was sent to sea'. The 'General Character and Behavioural' column had the word 'Good' written against his name.

Admissions Register of Cardigan Workhouse showing Margaret, David and Frances admitted on 31st October 1893 - *ref CBG/76 reproduced by permission of Ceredigion Archives, Aberystwyth*

Their father James was at sea during this time and it's not known when news of his wife's death reached him or if he ever returned to St Dogmaels to see his children. He remained at sea at least until 1908 and probably beyond that date, not having given any support financially or otherwise to any of his children. He later settled in the North East of England, re-married, and began a second family having seemingly abandoned his first.

His thirteen-year-old son David Thomas was discharged from the workhouse on 4 March 1903 and no time was wasted getting him on board his first ship. By the 9th he had signed on as ordinary seaman on the Liverpool registered barque the *Craigisla*. During the following seven years David sailed on three sail and six steam vessels, clocking up nearly six of these years actually at sea. What an experience it must have been for him from life in the workhouse to sailing the world's oceans. All these ships were employed in the foreign trade. In 1910 David became a second mate of a steam ship, passing his examination in the port of Cardiff. On this application form he gave his permanent address as 12 Williams Row, Cardigan and describes his personal description as 5ft 5in tall, fair complexion, brown hair and grey eyes.

David Thomas James who died in Shanghai in 1935

Little is known of his life during the following few years. He did sail throughout the First World War, and at one time was in charge of a trooper conveying men to Basra during the Mesopotamian campaign. He was mentioned in dispatches and awarded the 'Oak Leaf Emblem' in recognition of his actions. It was around about the end of the First World War that David went to work in the Far East for the firm of Butterfield & Swire, a trading company that had been established there since the middle of the 1800's with offices in Shanghai and Hong Kong. David sailed on their vessels, trading along the China coast.

Throughout his life David had always felt the pangs of 'hiraeth' (a welsh word for longing, nostalgia and home sickness rolled into one) for his beloved home country of Wales, despite his childhood being spent in the workhouse there. Unsurprisingly then he returned to St Dogmaels as often as he could on leave and it was on one of these visits that he married Annie Mary Ellen Davies, as already mentioned.

They married in the spring of 1920 in Cardigan and almost immediately David took his new wife back with him to the Far East to live. For Annie, I imagine, this was a very different and strange lifestyle compared with that of St Dogmaels. She settled down very well to Far East life but returned home to give birth to both their children, Frances Patricia in 1922 and David Fredrick in 1926. In 1925 David Thomas James joined the Shanghai Licensed Pilot Association where he became a well-respected pilot on the great Yangtze River. It was in Shanghai that they lived out the remainder of their time in the Far East. In the summer of 1935 David, Annie and the children returned to St Dogmaels for a holiday.

David returned to Shanghai early due to work commitments, Annie and the children stayed on in St Dogmaels, enjoying the Welsh hospitality and fully intending to re-join David in the New Year. Unfortunately, again disaster struck this family for David died suddenly soon after returning to Shanghai. The following article was published in the Cardigan and Tivyside Advertiser on Friday 7 February 1936, which best describes David and Annie's lifestyle and work in the Far East :

"DIED IN SHANGHAI – CARDIGAN CAPTAIN'S COLLAPSE IN LAUNCH

On December 27th last, the sad news reached Cardigan that Capt. DT James, whose wife and two children reside at Haulfryn, Gwbert Road, had died suddenly that morning at Shanghai, where he was a river/sea pilot. It was ascertained on medical evidence that he died from a clot of blood on the valves of the heart.
We have now received a copy of "The North China Daily News," containing the following account of his death and funeral:
Shanghai shipping circles were shocked yesterday at the news of the death early in the morning of Captain DT James, licensed pilot, as

he was going on duty. A member of the Shanghai Licensed Pilots Association, Captain James left the office at about 9.10am and appeared to be in his normal state of good health as he said good-bye to Captain JW Carle, manager of the Association before leaving for the pilot launch.

Ten minutes later however the laodah (crew) of the launch ran into the office and said that Captain James had collapsed a few minutes after he had boarded the launch. Captain Carle immediately went down to the boat and found Captain James lying on a settee in the cabin. An ambulance was hastily summoned, and he was taken to the General Hospital, but he was found to be dead on arrival.

A native of St. Dogmaels, where he was born some 45 years ago, the late Captain James was a sailor of the old school, receiving his apprenticeship in various square-rigged sailing ships. He first came out to China about twenty years ago and joined Messrs Butterfield & Squire's coastal fleet as master,

During the Great War Captain James was in command of a trooper conveying men to Basra during the drive in Mesopotamia. In 1926 he joined the Shanghai Licensed Pilot's Association, and only returned to Shanghai at the end of October this year after having been on home leave in his beloved Wales.

POPULAR EVERYWHERE

A member of the St. David's Society, he served on the committee of this association at various periods during the past few years, being noted for his capacity for doing a great deal of work without any ostentatious display. Although of a quiet and retiring nature, the late Captain James was very well known and universally liked in Shanghai, and was a popular member of the French Club, the Shanghai Club and the Mercantile Marine Officer's Club, which he joined in June 1926, being proposed by Captain E Budgen and seconded by Captain F H Jenne, both members of the same pilot's association as Captain James.

THE FUNERAL

The remains of the late Captain David Thomas James were interred in Hungjao Road Cemetery in the presence of a large attendance. Rev

H G Newsham of the Union Church conducted the service. Captain Carle and Mr Eric Davies were the chief mourners, representing the deceased's family at present at home. The pallbearer's were members of the Shanghai Licensed Pilot's Association. A beautiful Sheaf from his wife and a cross from his children, Patsy and Freddy, were lowered into the grave with the casket. Many people attended the funeral and also sent beautiful floral tributes, a testament as to how well respected Captain James was."

Annie was understandably devastated to hear of her husband's death. Her son, David Fredrick, was sent to live with his uncle Lewis Picton in Cardiff for a short period of time to allow his mother to recover from the terrible shock. David had the opportunity to holiday in China in recent times and while in Shanghai visited Hungjao Road Cemetery to pay his respects to his late father. Unfortunately Chairman Mao's Red Guards had destroyed many of the foreign gravestones during their Communist uprising in 1966-7, including his father's. David Thomas James's death ended this family's association with the sea

.

William Phillip, John and Mary Davies' seventh child

William Phillip Davies m. Elizabeth Anne Evans (widow)
1842-1908   abt.1843-?

|

Martha.A.Evans

|

Lizzie.G.Evans

CHAPTER 7

William Phillip – the seventh child of John and Mary Davies

William Phillip was born in 1842 and naturally, like all of John and Mary's children was brought up in Panteg. He was the youngest of their three sons and followed his father and his brothers into the seafaring life. Although he spent his whole working life at sea and became a master mariner, unfortunately for me as a researcher he did not apply for or take any Board of Trade examination to become one.

Consequently there are no records of when or on which ship he began his sailing career. One thing is certain, there was no shortage of ships to choose from in Cardigan and St Dogmaels in those days on which he could have learned his trade. It could be surmised that he did this on his father's ship the *Thetis,* as did his brother Evan, but there is no proof of this.

As previously mentioned, in 1865 his father sold the *Thetis* and in its place bought the 34-ton smack *Ellen Owens,* an ideal vessel for coastal trading. This I believe was not a replacement to enable his father to carry on sailing, he being sixty-three years old and now the landlord of the 'Sailors Home', but was for his son William to carry on the Davies family business in St Dogmaels and Cardigan. This it appears he did very successfully throughout his lifetime.

After her purchase William became master of the *Ellen Owens.* At first she was employed in the busy trade between Cardigan and Bristol and in the period 1 July to 31 December 1866, made eight voyages between the two ports, probably with general goods. The crew on these voyages were: William himself as master, mate another William Davies, from Fishguard, and seventeen-year-old John Davies from Cardigan. In the second half of 1871 *Ellen Owens* was as usual trading from her homeport of Cardigan along the Pembrokeshire and South Wales coast to Saundersfoot, Milford and Swansea for coal and culm. Her Account of Voyages and Crew, documenting all destinations and cargo carried for the first six months of 1884, sums up her working life during and after the time William was her master:

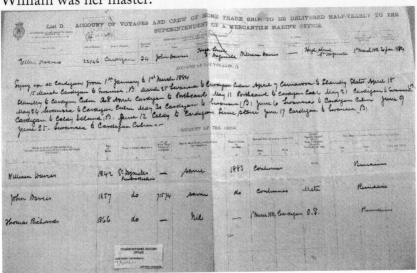

Account of Voyages and Crew for the ship 'Ellen Owens' showing William Davies as Master and his father John Davies as her Managing Owner. The Account also shows her ports visited and cargo carried during the period 1st March and 30th June 1884 - *Pembrokeshire Archives, Haverfordwest*

Ports visited and cargoes carried:

From	To	Cargo
Cardigan	Swansea	Ballast
Swansea	Cardigan	Culm
Cardigan	Caernarfon	Ballast
Caernarfon	Llanelli	Slates
Llanelli	Cardigan	Culm
Cardigan	Porthcawl	Ballast
Porthcawl	Cardigan	Coal
Cardigan	Swansea	Ballast
Swansea	Cardigan	Culm

Cardigan	Swansea	Ballast
Swansea	Cardigan	Culm
Cardigan	Caldey Island	Ballast
Caldey Island	Cardigan	Limestone
Cardigan	Swansea	Ballast
Swansea	Cardigan	Culm

The *Ellen Owens* was lying up in Cardigan until 15 March and arrived in Cardigan on 30 June.

These were a busy few months for this little vessel but typical of her work. With the exception of the occasional visit to the ports of Bristol and Dublin, all other ports visited were confined to the coast of Wales, transporting cargoes of coal, culm, limestone and slates. As an example the Account book of Williamston Quarries on the river Cleddau records that William Davies, Captain of the smack *Ellen Owens* of Cardigan, did purchase and load at the cost of £3. 15s. per 50 tons of limestone on 8 July 1872.

Four years later on 20 May 1876 the exact same transaction was recorded, the price per 50 tons had gone up to £4. 3s., an increase of 10 percent. In the spring of 1871, when the national census was taken, the *Ellen Owens* was in Portmadoc Harbor with William her master and two crew members. Ten years later in 1881 she was at the port of Swansea again with a crew of three. William and his father John certainly made the *Ellen Owens* earn her keep.

William had always lived with his parents and it appears, from documents I have researched, he was very close to his father. I'm sure then that his father, now getting on in years, would have welcomed the news that his forty-four-year-old son was to be married. This he did in the late spring of 1886, to Elizabeth Evans from Newport, Pembrokeshire.

This must have been a happy time for the family, lifting everyone's spirits. Sadly though these high spirits were not to last very much longer, especially for William, for just a few months later on 30 July 1886 his father died. At least his father had the comfort of knowing his son had someone to love and share the rest of his life with.

Elizabeth Evans was a widow when she married William. Her former husband Abraham Evans had been employed as a coastguard in Newport. In 1881 he drowned in a boating accident, leaving her with a three-year-old daughter Martha Anna and six-month-old Lizzie Gertrude, who sadly died in 1885. This must have left her mother devastated once again.

Many young widows and widowers in those days often found a partner to support or help to look after their families. Perhaps this was the case with Elizabeth and William's relationship. We will never know for sure but they did live out the rest of their lives happily together. Martha Anna also lived at home until William's death.

William needed to find a home for his new ready-made little family. In October 1887 he and his new wife purchased Angorfa, a house situated in High Street, St Dogmaels, for £120 from William James, a butcher, and his wife Mary. William and Elizabeth's names and signatures were on the deeds of Angorfa signifying that they owned the house jointly.

When William inherited *Ellen Owens*, and all her gear and herring nets from his father, he was now also her principal owner and master. He continued to sail and trade in the usual way until the middle of the 1890s when he was in his mid-fifties. He had been at sea all of his working life and now had decided that it was time for him to sit back and give others a chance. He remained the owner of the *Ellen Owens* but employed other masters to sail her.

For example, in 1896 Evan Lloyd of Penwhelp, St Dogmaels was her master and in 1902 two masters were employed, David Rees and John Isaac, also of St Dogmaels. In 1905 William sold the *Ellen Owens* to Thomas Jones of Aberayron. It must have been such a wrench for him to sell the little vessel that had been his pride and joy.

He had been her master for thirty years and her sole owner for half of that time but at his age had little choice. In his time he had sailed over the bar at Poppit and negotiated his way up the River Tivy to Cardigan literally hundreds of times and would have known every twist and turn of this difficult estuary.

There may have been another reason that influenced William to give up sailing the *Ellen Owens* in his mid fifties, because at around that time he held the office of surveyor[1] under The Aberporth Mutual Ship Insurance Company. He was very successful in floating a number of sunken vessels, the most notable being that of the *Brothers,* which sank off Skomer Island in 1891. This vessel was filled with petroleum barrels and towed back to Cardigan by the SS *Seaflower.* He also in 1898 raised the *Mouse,* which had sunk off the Black Rocks at Poppit laden with coal. Perhaps he found that both running professions simultaneously a little too much.

He obviously didn't know it when he bought her in 1905 but Thomas Jones tenancy of the *Ellen Owens* was not to be as long or as lucky as William's had been; in fact it lasted less than two years. In 1907 whilst sailing out of Swansea with a cargo of culm for Aberaeron and when still in the confines of Swansea Bay she was in collision with the West Hartlepool registered SS *Kirkstall,* and foundered. Both Thomas Jones, who was her master and her one other crewmember were saved.

In September 1908 William died at home, the cause of death given as gangrene of his foot and leg. How much use he made over the years of the herring nets that his father left him in his will is not known but it must have been some, for his occupation as recorded on his Death Certificate was a fisherman. He is buried with his parents in the St Dogmaels Parish Church graveyard. It was later reported in his obituary in the Tivyside that he and his little vessel were both well known and well respected.

1 *A Marine Surveyor's responsibilities amongst other things are inspecting and evaluating various vessels to ensure that they meet the designated classification and regulations. In the case of accidents they may be called upon to investigate the causes and be an expert witness and in such cases the question of appropriate marine insurance is reviewed.*

Anne, John and Mary Davies' eighth child

Anne Davies m. Lewis Davies
1848-1906   1843-1909

CHAPTER 8

Anne – the eighth child of John and Mary Davies

Anne was born in 1848, the last of John and Mary's children. She naturally lived at home with her parents during her formative years but by the time she had reached the age of twenty-one she had met her husband to be. He was twenty-six-year-old Lewis Davies of Penrallt-y-dre Farm, also in St Dogmaels. They married on 10 July 1869 at Tyrhos Chapel, Cilgerran.

Anne may have been the last of the Panteg children to be born but was the first not to marry into a mariner family. Lewis's family had been farming Penrallt-y-dre since about 1814 but he did not choose to follow in his family footsteps. The 1861 census shows his occupation as carpenter, and eight years later, when he married Anne, on the marriage certificate he was recorded as a contractor and builder. It seems that Lewis was going places and had ambition.

After the wedding this young couple moved to a house in High Street, St Dogmaels. Twelve years later the 1881 census shows them still living there and Lewis was recorded as a master joiner employing six hands. He was doing very well indeed.

If things were going well for Lewis and Anne in 1881, things did not go well back at Penrallt-y-dre. Lewis' seventy-three-year-old mother Mary and her fifty-eight-year-old brother John were now running the farm. In December of that year they both died within two days of each other, leaving the family with a dire problem, as they were the only two of the Penrallt Davies' still living there at that time. The solution was for Lewis and Anne to move back to and

145

to farm Penrallt-y-dre. This they did and continued to do so until about 1903. It's not known if Lewis continued with the contracting business as well as farming at Penrallt-y-dre.

As previously mentioned Anne and Lewis in 1891 took in and brought up their great niece and nephew Annie Mary Ellen and Lewis Picton, who were literally babes in arms, after the untimely death of their mother. Anne was in her early forties and had no children of her own, so this was a very brave, kind and generous act indeed and to her credit she brought them up as their own with warmth, love and kindness, a fact conveyed by Annie Mary Ellen in later life to her son David.

Also living on the farm in 1901 was John George Owens, nephew of Anne and Lewis. He was of course also uncle of the two little children. This perhaps suggests that Penrallt-y-dre was a warm, welcoming, and cosy place where everyone was welcomed.

Lewis in the 1890s did have interests outside the farming of Penrallt-y-dre. Glen K Johnson in his book 'St Dogmaels Uncovered' points out that Lewis in 1897 was recorded as a Rural District Councillor. About 1903, probably after leaving Penrallt-y-dre, Lewis became the landlord of the 'Webley' public house situated a mile or so down river from St Dogmaels.

In September of 1906, Anne, the kind and generous great aunt, died, to the great sadness I'm sure of Lewis and their two adopted children. Just three years later, in May of 1909 Lewis himself died in his mid sixties. Both are buried in the St Dogmaels Parish Church graveyard. His obituary in The Cardigan and Tivyside Advertiser describes his life as follows:

"An old inhabitant of St. Dogmaels passed away at his residence, The Poppit House, after a lengthened illness. Mr Lewis Davies, formerly in business as a builder and contractor. Mr Davies had been a member of the Board of Guardians and the St. Dogmaels rural District Councillor for years, and was universally respected at St. Dogmaels and in the district at large. The deceased, who was 66 years of age, had also been a member of the old School Board, and he and his predecessors

had resided and farmed at Penrallt for close upon a hundred years."

Webley Arms circa 1906. The man is believed to be Lewis Davies and the girl second from right Annie Mary Ellen (this public house at one time was also known as Poppit House).

Voyage of Discovery

In the late 1990s I set about researching my family history on my father's side. I chose this branch to research simply because I knew very little about this side of my family. I did know my father's twin brother and his sister, my uncle and aunt, also their children, my cousins, but that is as far as it went.

I was helped along the way by many kind people, most I have already mentioned who not only gave up their time enthusiastically to talk to me about their recollections of the old days but also produced photographs and family bibles etc. which helped me very much to get the feel of the family. My cousin James Lodwig Davies in particular generously allowed me access to the work he had already done on the subject, for which I am eternally grateful.

After some four years or so of my research it became clear that this family during the nineteenth and into the twentieth century was very involved with the sea and the maritime life, not only of Cardigan and South Ceredigion's coastal ports and landing places but also the oceans of the world. Their lives on those great sailing ships to far away mysterious destinations were often thought of as perhaps adventurous, exciting or even romantic, but in reality they had much to endure, cut off from their families and normal life ashore on long voyages for months or even years.

The conditions on board were pretty awful to say the least. They would have slept in cramped conditions on boarded bunks or on straw mattresses if they were lucky, sometimes perhaps in a hammock. Everything they touched would be cold and wet and the food not only in short supply but also disgusting to eat, such as weevil-ridden hard tack, salted meat and maybe a bit of cheese.

They faced the daily dangers of the sea and the weather. Climbing the rigging to trim the sails in all weather conditions was not for the meek, be it wet, cold, icy, stormy, windy or in the blazing hot sunshine of the tropics, but up they had to go. They did all this for very poor pay to boot.

It was an extremely dangerous occupation as examples in this book have shown. They had to be tough to survive. Most mariners in this family for example made a lifelong career of seafaring, so what made them return time and again to the sea and to what seems to us today as intolerable conditions in their working lives? Have we missed something? Perhaps there was a grain of truth in the thought that somehow it really was adventurous, exciting, and romantic and worth enduring.

What is striking about the mariners in this family is that they were a very ambitious lot. They went to sea at a very young age, some at the age of twelve. They learnt their trade and as soon as they felt able they strived to become a second mate, then first mate and the final goal of master mariner. The majority did reach this eminent position, and who could blame them for wanting to aspire to such heights? Ship's captains have always been held in high regard and are much-respected pillars of the community. In the early years they bought shares in ships, owning ships in their own right and managed the business of trade and cargo. There was much to admire about these seafarers.

During the course of my research I always wondered what life might have been like on board these ships for those mariners. I would have relished the opportunity, if only for one day to have joined the Swansea barque *Evangeline* on her voyage from New Orleans to Rouen France in 1880, when Captain Evan Davies of Mount Pleasant was her master. Unfortunately of course that time has long gone and my wish will never be granted but in 2008 I discovered the charity 'The Jubilee Sailing Trust', an organization that operates two tall sailing ships, the *Lord Nelson* and *Tenacious,* so my next best wish of sailing as crew member of a modern day barque was granted.

I have joined the *Tenacious* as a crew member on three voyages so far, from Southampton to Las Palmas, Milford Haven to Barcelona and Bahamas to Bermuda, three most memorable voyages.

Each voyage has been an unforgettable adventure. The Jubilee Sailing Trust is a charity that promotes the integration of able and disabled persons to sail together as 'voyage crew'. Both ships are adapted for disabled people and fitted with lifts and safe anchoring points for wheelchairs etc. Each will take part as equals in all work and duties in the sailing of the ship whether it be keeping watch by day and night, helming the ship, bracing the sails, trimming the sails, helping in the galley or even cleaning the heads (toilets) also much more besides.

The phrase 'voyage crew' refers to the crew for one particular voyage who do all the work needed to sail the ship from A to B under the expert guidance of a small but very experienced permanent crew.

Sea water washing over the deck of the bark 'Tenacious' whilst sailing south across the Bay of Biscay in heavy weather

I have many memorable moments of the voyages that I have sailed; here is a brief account of a few:

While sailing south in the Bay of Biscay we were hit by three days of stormy weather. The *Tenacious'* bow rose into the air only to fall again onto the next wave with a huge splash, when she keeled over some of the wave would wash thousands of gallons of water pouring over her decks, an exhilarating sight. Everyone on deck wore safety harnesses of course and clipped onto safety rails, a luxury the old sailors did not have. At meal times sticky mats were placed under plates of food or else the plates would swoosh off the table in a jiff, such was the violent movement of the vessel.

Harbour stowing the course sail on the main mast before entering the port of Cadiz, southwest Spain. Author fourth from left

It was always exciting after only three weeks to see our destination appearing on the horizon, whatever must it have been like to spend months at sea? Sailing on modern day barques, only in a small way, replicates sailing ships of the 1800s but nevertheless it is a fantastic experience and I recommend it for anyone whether able bodied or disabled to take the opportunity.

The Jubilee Sailing Trust sail from UK ports in the summer for periods of one day and upward, and from warmer climates such as the Mediterranean and Caribbean in the winter months.

REFERENCES

Davies, Peter B S - Deadly Perils (Published by Merrivale)

Evans, S Idris - Brasluns o Hanes Eglwys Annibynnol Bethel Trewyddel 1861- 1991

Davies, Donald (Ed.) - 'Those were the days' A History of Cardigan, the locality and its people. Volumes 1 & 2 (Edited and Published by 'The Cardigan and Tivy-Side Advertiser)

Fenton, R S - Cambrian Coasters, Steam and Motor Coasters owners of North and West Wales (Kendal, World Ship Society 1989)

Greenlaw, Joanna - Swansea Copper Barques and Cape Horners

Herber, Mark - Ancestral Trails (second edition - Sutton Publishing Ltd in association with Society of Genealogists)

Johnson, Glen K - St Dogmaels, Uncovered Heritage of a Parish

Jenkins, J Geraint - The Maritime Heritage of Some Southern Ceredigion Villages

Jenkins, J Geraint - Maritime Heritage The Ships and Seamen of Southern Ceredigion (Gomer Press, Llandysul, Dyfed)

153

Jenkins, J Geraint - Welsh Ships and Sailing Men, translated by Martin Davies (MOROL Institute of Welsh Maritime Heritage Studies)

Larn, R & B - 'Shipwreck' index of the British Isles

Lewis, W J - 'The Gateway to Wales' A History of Cardigan (Published by the Cultural Services Dept. Dyfed County Council in 1999)

Passmore, Sue - Farmers and Figureheads (Grosvenor House Publishing Ltd)

Thomas, Peter - Strangers from a Secret Land (University of Toronto Press, Toronto, Buffalo, London)

Winfield, Rif - The 50 Gun Ships (Chatham Publishing – London)

The Cardigan and Tivy-Side Advertiser Archives 1866-1940

Volume 5 - Shipwreck index of Wales and the West Coast 2000

Volume 6 - Shipwreck index of Ireland 2002

THE AUTHOR

I was born in 1943 in the little village of Bryngwyn in the parish of Brongwyn situated in the South of the County of Ceredigion. I went to schools in the neighbouring village of Beulah and then St Mary's Secondary Modern School in Cardigan. At the age of seventeen and in search of a little adventure I joined the Royal Air Force and moved away from Bryngwyn. I met my wife Rita in Suffolk while serving in the Royal Air Force and have lived and worked there ever since but have returned home many times every year. It still holds a very special place in my heart.

APPENDIX - SHIP SHAPES

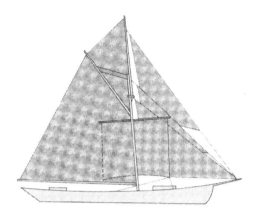

Sloop

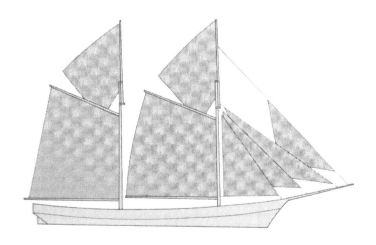

Schooner

Brig

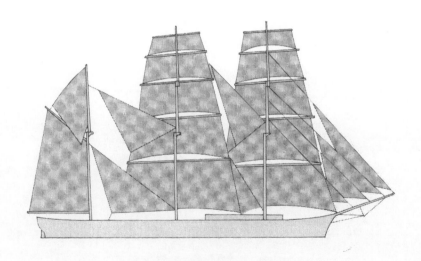

3 Masted Barque

Printed in Great Britain
by Amazon.co.uk, Ltd.,
Marston Gate.